CULTURE SMART!

LITHUANIA

Lara Belonogoff

·K·U·P·E·R·A·R·D·

First published in Great Britain 2007
by Kuperard, an imprint of Bravo Ltd
59 Hutton Grove, London N12 8DS
Tel: +44 (0) 20 8446 2440 Fax: +44 (0) 20 8446 2441
www.culturesmartguides.com
Inquiries: sales@kuperard.co.uk

Culture Smart! is a registered trademark of Bravo Ltd

Distributed in the United States and Canada
by Random House Distribution Services
1745 Broadway, New York, NY 10019
Tel: +1 (212) 572-2844 Fax: +1 (212) 572-4961
Inquiries: csorders@randomhouse.com

Copyright © 2007 Kuperard

Series Editor Geoffrey Chesler
Design Bobby Birchall

ISBN 978 1 85733 350 3

British Library Cataloguing in Publication Data
A CIP catalogue entry for this book is available from the
British Library

Printed in Malaysia

This book is available for special discounts for bulk purchases for
sales promotions or premiums. Special editions, including
personalized covers, excerpts of existing books, and corporate
imprints, can be created in large quantities for special needs.

For more information in the U.S.A. write to Special
Markets/Premium Sales, 1745 Broadway, MD 6–2, New York,
NY 10019 or e-mail specialmarkets@randomhouse.com.

In the United Kingdom contact Kuperard publishers at the
above address.

Cover image: White clock tower, Cathedral Square, Vilnius.
Travel Ink/Jeremy Phillips
Images reproduced by permission of the Lithuanian Tourist Board on the
following pages: 13, 57, 63, 64, 65, 117, 125, 126, 130, 132, and 133
Images on pages 81 © Wojsyl and 136 © Mantas Indrasius

CultureSmart!Consulting and **Culture Smart!** guides have both
contributed to and featured regularly in the weekly travel program
"Fast Track" on BBC World TV.

About the Author

LARA BELONOGOFF is an American travel writer and journalist who has lived and worked in Lithuania for a number of years. She has a B.A. Hons in English Literature from the University of California, Berkeley, and an MFA in Creative Writing from New School University, New York. Lara has worked in Central and Eastern Europe as an editor and writer for the authoritative *In Your Pocket* city guide series and in the USA. She currently lives in San Francisco and is the supervisor of the copywriting department for Gilbert Guide and unofficially works as a promoter for Lithuanian tourism.

Other Countries in the Culture Smart! Series

- Argentina
- Australia
- Austria
- Belgium
- Botswana
- Brazil
- Britain
- Chile
- China
- Costa Rica
- Cuba
- Czech Republic
- Denmark
- Estonia
- Egypt
- Finland
- France

- Germany
- Greece
- Guatemala
- Hong Kong
- Hungary
- India
- Indonesia
- Ireland
- Israel
- Italy
- Japan
- Kenya
- Korea
- Mexico
- Morocco
- Netherlands
- New Zealand

- Norway
- Panama
- Peru
- Philippines
- Poland
- Portugal
- Russia
- Singapore
- South Africa
- Spain
- Sweden
- Switzerland
- Thailand
- Turkey
- Ukraine
- USA
- Vietnam

Other titles are in preparation. For more information, contact: info@kuperard.co.uk

The publishers would like to thank **CultureSmart!**Consulting for its help in researching and developing the concept for this series.

contents

contents

Map of Lithuania

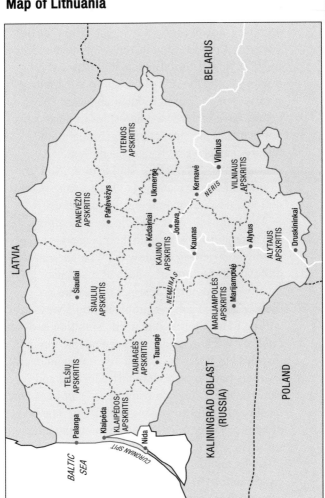

introduction

Lithuania has been one of Europe's best-kept
secrets. Trapped inside the Soviet Union for fifty
years until proclaiming its renewed independence
in 1990, this historic Baltic nation has lost no
time rejoining the rest of the world. A certain
resolve can be seen in Lithuanian faces. The
people have endured the hardships of a harsh
political and physical climate. Throughout its
history names were changed as the state was
constantly under attack or subjugation. And yet
Lithuanians have managed to keep a fairly sunny
outlook, despite the long years of adversity.

The Lithuanians as a whole are welcoming,
and happy to show visitors their country's many
charms. On getting to know them better, you will
discover deeper qualities such as resilience,
loyalty, and resourcefulness; Lithuanians are
usually good at solving problems and always
willing to help a friend in need. Ambition and
modesty work in tandem to keep people moving
forward but never putting on airs. Lithuanian city
dwellers tend to be both highly educated and
well-rounded; they can name species of trees and
mushrooms with surprising familiarity. The love
of nature is very much a part of the Lithuanian
soul. They have a profound romantic streak, often
offset by humor. These qualities on an individual
scale can lead to thought-provoking
conversations over a cup of coffee that can last

for hours, and in the grander scheme of things are what propel the nation forward.

Today Lithuania is flourishing as one of the newer EU member states. The economy is growing steadily. The tourism industry has opened up to allow vacationers a chance to discover its beautiful old towns and pristine countryside. However, a great deal of the country's charm is best viewed by going off the beaten path, or putting one's head into courtyards to see what the locals are doing. Visitors staying for prolonged periods often leave the country with the sense that they have found a second home in the friends they have made.

Culture Smart! Lithuania sets out to explain the nuances and protocols of Lithuanian society so that you can avoid social faux pas and get closer to the people. It offers key insights into the cultural and historical background, and advice to guide you through different types of business and social occasions—but reading this book is just the beginning of a journey. The true adventure starts in Lithuania, sitting in a Vilnius café on a breezy summer's day, talking philosophy late at night over a pint of the delicious domestic beer, or spending a Saturday by a lake cooking *shashlik*. It is only in conversations with people and exploration of the country that any true understanding of the Lithuanians can be reached.

Key Facts

Official Name	The Republic of Lithuania (*Lietuvos Respublika*)	
Capital City	Vilnius	Pop. 553,904
Major Cities	Kaunas, Klaipėda, Šiauliai, Panevėžys, Alytus, Marijampolė	
Borders	Latvia, Belarus, Poland, Kaliningrad (Russia)	
Area	25,173 square miles (65,200 square kilometers)	
Terrain	Mostly low-lying, with many forests, lakes and rivers	
Climate	Mix of continental and maritime	January average is 23.4°F (-4.8°C). July average is 63°F (17.2°C). The average rainfall is 31 inches (800 mm).
Currency	The Lithuanian litas (LTL), with the euro coming in 2008	
Population	3,431,000	
Ethnic Makeup	Lithuanian (85%) Poles (6.7%) Russians (6%) Belarusians (1.1%) Others (1.2%)	
Ethnographic Regions	Žemaitija (west), Aukštaitija (center and east), Suvalkija (below the Nemunas River), and Dzūkija (south)	There are cultural and language differences between these regions.

Language	Lithuanian	
Religion	Roman Catholic (79%), Russian Orthodox (4.9 %), Protestants (1.9%), and other, comprised of Judaism, Karaims, and Muslim (1.6%)	
Government	Parliamentary democracy since 1991	The head of state is the president, elected for 5 years. Head of government is the prime minister. The parliament (the Seimas) has 141 members, elected for 4 years.
Media	There are 2 state-owned and 6 independent TV channels. *Lietuvos rytas* is the biggest daily newspaper, *Respublika* the second largest, trailed by *Lietuvos aidas*.	New services include ELTA, a former government agency that is now privatized, and the Baltic News Service (BNS), which covers all three Baltic countries.
Electricity	220 volts/50 Hz, with two-pronged plug	
Video/TV	PAL/SECAM system	
Telephone	The country code is +370.	The city code for Vilnius is 5. In Lithuania, dial 8 and then the city code plus the number.
Time Zone	Eastern European Time (GMT+2) and in summer (GMT+3)	

chapter one

LAND & PEOPLE

GEOGRAPHY

The largest of the Baltic states, Lithuania is bounded to the north by Latvia, to the east by Belarus, to the south by Poland and the Kaliningrad area of Russia, and to the west by the Baltic Sea. It is a gently undulating land of great natural beauty, made green and fertile by an abundance of water. The visitor will find it nearly impossible to avoid some rain, whether a light spring shower or a heavy fall downpour. About a third of the countryside is forested, and there are thousands of small lakes, mainly in the east, and hundreds of rivers. The largest river is the Nemunas, which snakes northward from Belarus past the city of Kaunas, where it turns west and follows the border with Kaliningrad before emptying into the Baltic Sea. The Neris River is the largest tributary of the Nemunas and flows through the city of Vilnius before meeting the Nemunas in Kaunas.

Lithuania stretches across 25,173 square miles (65,200 sq. kilometers), and has a maritime to continental climate. Sand dunes along the coast give way to coastal lowlands. The lowlands run north to south, with gentle hills in the west, and portions contain wetlands and rich loam. To their east are the Žemaitija highlands. The highest terrain is in the eastern and southern parts of the country, with the highest point being Mount Juozapinė at 965 feet (294 meters) above sea level. What Lithuanians refer to as hills or mountains would, in most other parts of the world, be called knolls or small rises. A sandy plain encircles most of the southeastern border with Belarus.

This varied natural landscape is intersected by some of the best maintained roads in the region, making travel by car a pleasure—if the weather cooperates. Most visitors to the country spend time in one of the three large cities or at the coast. Vilnius, the only Baltic capital not situated on the seaside, is a glorious example of Baroque architecture in a seemingly too northern setting. Kaunas, the second largest city, is considered the most "Lithuanian" of cities in the republic and its residents tend to think of themselves as its intellectual and cultural elite. Klaipėda (formerly Memel) has a distinct port feel to it, and its timber-

framed *Fachwerk* houses remain, reminding one of the past German influence.

Perhaps Lithuania's most beautiful feature is the northern coast, with its punctuation mark of the Curonian Spit. A designated national park, this is a long, curving peninsula of sand dunes and pine forests, a mile wide and 60 miles (97 km) long, stretching from the Lithuanian republic into the Russian enclave of Kaliningrad, and forming a great lagoon between it and the mainland.

A BRIEF HISTORY
The Unification of the State

The ancient Balts were speakers of an Indo-European language who settled in the areas between the Vistula and Daugava rivers and the Baltic Sea. Most scholars believe that the Baltic tribes settled permanently in present-day Lithuania and Latvia in around 700 BCE. The Lithuanian state first took shape when Grand Duke Mindaugas united the pagan tribes to resist invasion by the German crusading orders—the Teutonic Knights, based in Prussia, and the Livonian Brothers of the Sword, based in Latvia. He adopted Christianity in 1251, and was crowned King of Lithuania on July 6, 1253.

The Reign of Gediminas

Mindaugas's coronation as the first and only king of Lithuania created awareness of a Lithuanian state outside the country, but it was the reign of Grand Duke Gediminas (1316–41) that consolidated it. Kernavė, a pagan shrine and home to a series of five hill forts, was the first capital of Lithuania—if not in name, then in practice. Gediminas moved the capital to Trakai after seeing the area while on a hunting trip. A Gothic castle, which has undergone quite a few reconstructions, still stands there today on an island in the lake.

According to tradition Gediminas founded the city of Vilnius after having a dream on the site of the present-day Vilnius Castle. One day, while hunting deep in the woods, which today are central Vilnius, he managed to fell an aurochs (wild ox). After killing the creature he took a nap in the Šventaragis Valley, at the foot of Vilnius's Castle Hill, and in a dream he saw an iron wolf, which howled with the force of a hundred wolves. Later a high priest interpreted this as meaning that a great city—as resilient and forceful as an iron wolf with a far-reaching cry—would be built on the spot where the dream occurred. All three areas are important signposts in the developing Lithuanian consciousness, in that the pagan roots of Kernavė are linked with the fantastical elements of Trakai, and forged into the shining new capital of Vilnius. Gediminas's progress also points to a certain characteristic of Lithuanian people—they enjoy the outdoors and are constantly looking for a piece of land that is a little better than what they have.

After Mindaugas's death, Lithuania reverted to paganism, and the Teutonic Knights resumed their systematic raiding. In response Gediminas signed treaties with the city of Riga in 1323, and formed a union with Poland in 1325 by marrying his daughter Aldona to the Polish king's son. Some historians think that his move from Trakai to Vilnius was a strategic one, as the latter was more easily defended. Gediminas made overtures to the Pope, holding out the prospect of his conversion, and in 1323 he invited monks, craftsmen, merchants, and men of every order and profession from various German towns to settle in Lithuania, sending out circular letters to the main Hansa cities offering work, privileges, and freedom to practice their religion to those willing to move to his new capital of Vilnius. Through alliances and conquest, he extended his rule eastward at the expense of Russia, at that time controlled by the Mongols, acquiring most of modern Belarus and Ukraine, and creating a Lithuanian empire that stretched from the Baltic toward the Black Sea.

Civil War

After Gediminas's death two of his sons, Algirdas and Kęstutis, seized power from their brother Jaunutis, the rightful heir, and divided the Grand Duchy between them. Algirdas suppressed the monasteries and fought in the east, even marching to Moscow—he twice surrounded the city, once in 1368 for three days and again in 1370 for eight days, but never attacked it. Meanwhile Kęstutis saw off the Teutonic Knights in the west. This arrangement worked well until Algirdas's death. After his pagan burial, complete with his horse and cloaked in a golden robe, his son Jogaila inherited his portion of the Grand Duchy.

Grand Duke Jogaila (1377–92) chose not to share power with his uncle, Kęstutis. He entered into a secret alliance against him with the Teutonic Order, and civil war followed. The order to kill Kęstutis was given—historians argue whether it was by Jogaila or by the convenient foil of his mother, Algirdas's Russian wife  Julijona, who was looking out for his interest. In any event, Kęstutis was strangled, but his son Vytautas escaped. This episode is often used to illustrate the point that Jogaila was duplicitous. Vytautas now vied with Jogaila for control of the Duchy, although the cousins halted their feuding in 1402 in order to expel the invading Teutonic Knights. (In 1390 Vilnius was burned almost to the ground, although the Knights did not succeed in taking the stone castle.)

Union with Poland

Lithuania and Poland were both threatened by the Teutonic Knights, and by the growing power of Muscovy, and an alliance was in their common interest. In 1385 Jogaila signed the Krėva or Krewo Union, by which, in return for converting to

Christianity, he would marry the underage Princess Jadwiga of Poland and Hungary and become King of Poland. In 1386 he was baptized, just as Mindaugas had been, and married, and the following year pagan Lithuania was converted. The marriage created a personal, dynastic union between Poland and Lithuania, and the new king moved to Kraków. Herein lies the source of the idea that Jogaila was duplicitous—many Lithuanians believe he was responsible for "selling" Lithuania to Poland. (To this day the name Jogaila is unpopular in Lithuania, but common in Poland.)

Vytautas, known as "the Great," ruled Lithuania from 1392 to 1430. In 1401 he secured the Union Treaty, signed in Vilnius, which guaranteed Lithuania's autonomy and equality. Formerly Prince, he now became Grand Duke of the Grand Duchy of Lithuania.

The Battle of Grünwald
Although Lithuania was now a Christian state and the Teutonic Knights had no further basis for attacking it, they continued to do so. The two sides seemed unequal: the well-trained and highly organized German knights were opposed by a motley crew of Poles, Lithuanians, and some Tatars and Bohemian Hussites. Nevertheless, in a

momentous battle on July 15, 1410—the Battle of Grünwald or Žalgiris, also known as the Tannenberg Battle—the Polish-Lithuanian army decisively defeated the Teutonic Knights.

Grand Duke Vytautas, who led the Lithuanian forces, is usually given more credit for the victory in the Lithuanian versions of history than his cousin Jogaila, who is favored by Polish accounts of the battle. (The popular Lithuanian belief is that Jogaila prayed for victory whereas Vytautas  fought for it.) In any case, the defeat was resounding, and even aided by some peasants who, armed with clubs, took to belaboring the enemy. By ridding the country of these invaders the Polish-Lithuanian Union enjoyed a long bout of prosperity and growth. By 1430, as it expanded from the Baltic to the Black Sea and approached Moscow, it seemed invincible. However, in the same year Vytautas died without an heir, and Polish influence in Lithuania grew stronger.

Polonization

In 1429, in the hope of splitting up the Polish-Lithuanian Union, the Holy Roman Emperor Sigismund had offered to crown Vytautas King of Lithuania. A crown made by Nuremberg goldsmiths was sent to arrive in Vilnius in time for the coronation on September 8, 1430. However, the convoy was stopped on the Polish-German border by members of the Polish nobility, who stole the crown and coronation documents, thereby thwarting Vytautas's attempt to walk away from the Union. Another crown was sent, but Vytautas died before it reached Lithuania. (This is still a sore point for Lithuanians, some of whom count the coronation date as a holiday, even though it never took place. Furthermore, during the period between the two world wars, when Lithuanian hatred of Poland hit a fever pitch, many boys were named Vytautas.)

The Jogaila (Jagiełło) dynasty continued until 1572, but as the Union grew in strength Lithuania's political and cultural role dwindled. Vilnius had little influence over Kraków, and the Lithuanian nobility began speaking Polish at court, so that in time Polish became the language of the educated classes and Lithuanian largely the language of the peasantry. This marginalization of Lithuania was slow but steady. However, there were also important cultural achievements during this time.

In the late 1500s Vilnius blossomed as craftsmen flooded into the city and made it their home. The architecture of Renaissance Italy that can be seen in Vilnius's many churches is the result of the marriage of an Italian princess, Bona Sforza, to Sigismund the Old (1506–1548), Grand Duke of Lithuania and King of Poland. Lithuanian literature written in Latin flourished, and the first handwritten and printed texts in the Lithuanian language emerged, beginning the formation of a written Lithuanian language.

The Union of Lublin

With the Union of Lublin in 1569 the Kingdom of Poland and Grand Duchy of Lithuania formed a new state: the Republic of the Two Nations, known as Poland-Lithuania or the Polish-Lithuanian Commonwealth. This lasted until the adoption by the Sejm (parliament) of the Constitution of May 3, 1791, which finally abolished the division of Poland and Lithuania. The Commonwealth covered not only the territories of what is now Poland and Lithuania, but also Belarus and Latvia, large parts of Ukraine and Estonia, and part of present-day western Russia. In 1696 Polish replaced Lithuanian as the official state language.

Partition and Russification

The power of the fractious Polish nobility increased at the expense of the crown, and the Polish-Lithuanian Commonwealth grew increasingly unstable. It soon came under attack from its powerful neighbors, Prussia, Russia, and Habsburg Austria. In three partitions, in 1772, 1793, and 1795, they divided the Commonwealth lands among themselves. Most of Lithuania fell to Imperial Russia and ceased to exist as a separate entity for more than a century. Vilnius became the third-largest city in the Russian Empire after Moscow and St. Petersburg.

In the early years of the nineteenth century, there were hopes that Lithuania might still be allowed some separate recognition by the Empire.

Napoleon's attempt to seize Moscow saw him crossing Lithuania in 1812. Many Lithuanians greeted him as a liberator; on his disastrous retreat thousands of French soldiers died near Vilnius from the freezing temperatures and lack of supplies. Estimates have nearly 30,000 French soldiers dying in the streets of Vilnius. After the French withdrawal, Tsar Nicholas I began an intensive program of Russification.

Digging Their Own Grave

In 2001 two mass grave sites containing the remains of soldiers from Napoleon's army were unearthed in Vilnius. The troops retreating from Moscow had few if any supplies and temperatures hovered around -22°F (-30°C). As men died from exposure, their bodies littering the city streets became a problem. Eventually, trenches that had been dug by the French on their way to Moscow were used as mass graves. Today a joint French and Lithuanian government-sponsored memorial stands at Antakalnis cemetery to commemorate their sacrifice.

Things stayed fairly quiet until 1831, when an uprising against the Russian Empire resulted in the closing of Vilnius University after staff and students were accused of organizing the rebellion. The crackdown that followed took away the last remaining rights from the state, which had retained some limited autonomy up to this point. Lithuania was erased from the maps, its territories referred to as the Northwest Region, the Lithuanian language could only be printed in Cyrillic characters, and many Catholic and Lutheran churches were closed. The 1863 uprising, in which both Lithuanians and Poles rose up against serfdom and for independence from Russia, was met with even greater ferocity; its Lithuanian organizers were hanged publicly in Vilnius's Lukiškių Square by General Muryavov, who was dubbed "the Hangman."

However, despite the loss of civil liberties and political power, some growth did occur in the late 1800s. For example, the city of Kaunas became a strategic base for the defense of the Empire's western frontiers. The Oginsky Canal, connecting the Nemunas and Dnieper rivers, was built, insuring that Kaunas also became an important commercial hub. In the second half of the nineteenth century, the port of Memel (Klaipėda), then part of Prussia, became a center for the publication of books printed in the Lithuanian language using the Latin alphabet—prohibited in the Russian Empire. The books were then smuggled over the border into Lithuania.

In the 1880s Lithuania developed an organized nationalist movement. During the Russia-wide revolutionary upsurge of

1905 a congress (Seimas) of Lithuanian
representatives demanded provincial autonomy.
During the First World War, occupation by
Germany in 1915 and the subsequent collapse
of the Russian imperial government enabled the
newly empowered Council of Lithuania to

proclaim an independent
republic on February 16,
1918, while still under
German control, and to
achieve independence
upon Germany's
surrender in
November 1918.

Independence

The German army had seized Vilnius in September
1915. In 1918 German troops began leaving the
southern part of the country and a new conflict
began. Ignoring the Lithuanian Council's
declaration of independence, both the Polish and the
Red Armies invaded, and each occupied Vilnius for
two distinct periods. At the end of the Polish-Soviet
war in 1921, Polish forces commanded by Marshal
Józef Piłsudski were able to hold on to Vilnius and
many lands south and west of the city. From 1920 to
1939 the area Poland occupied was renamed Middle
Lithuania, after a territory in the old Polish-
Lithuanian Commonwealth. Vilnius had many
Polish citizens, which remained the case until after
the start of the Second World War. During this
period Kaunas served as the interim capital of

sovereign Lithuania. Kaunas thrived as Art Deco and Bauhaus made their indelible marks on its architecture and the city became the cultural capital of the country, a position it still maintains to this day.

Soviet Lithuania

On August 23, 1939, Hitler and Stalin signed the notorious Molotov-Ribbentrop Pact, a "non-aggression treaty" with secret clauses that assigned each party spheres of influence in the Baltic area. Lithuania was initially assigned to Germany, but when it refused to join Nazi Germany in the attack on Poland, it was transferred to the Soviets later that year. In fall 1939 Soviet troops began to move into Lithuania on the pretext of fending off possible invading German forces. In July 1940 elections to the so-called People's Parliament were organized with only the collaborationist Communist Party of Lithuania nominating candidates. The new parliament declared Lithuania's will to join the Soviet Union and on August 3, 1941, the Supreme Council of the USSR "admitted" Lithuania into the Soviet Union. The Lithuanian Soviet Socialist Republic was created.

The first Soviet occupation was short, but brutal. Beginning on June 14, 1941, about 35,000 Lithuanian "enemies of the state" were deported to Siberian work camps or executed. Several thousand were killed in more than forty massacres around the country. Most of the people targeted in this systematic dismantling of the state were middle-class Lithuanians—teachers, students, wealthy farmers, the intelligentsia, and doctors. The idea was that this class of people posed the greatest threat to the implementation of the Soviet system of government. Frightened and shocked by these inhuman acts, Lithuanians watched for any possibility of liberation.

German Occupation

On June 22, 1941, Hitler invaded the Soviet Union. German troops entered Lithuania and many people welcomed them as liberators from Soviet domination. The retreating Soviet forces duly massacred Lithuanian political prisoners. The underground Lithuanian Activist Front used the opportunity to declare independence, and the newly proclaimed Lithuanian government tried to negotiate with Germany to grant Lithuania independence. The Germans had other plans, however, and gradually stripped the government of its powers. Lithuania, Latvia, and Estonia were incorporated into Greater Germany as the administrative unit of Ostland. The Lithuanian Activist Front was banned.

The Holocaust

The Nazis started the implementation of their "Final Solution" in Lithuania. There was a significant Jewish population in the Baltic region, of nearly 480,000 people. To these were added deportees from Austria, Germany, and elsewhere. The extermination of resident Jews began almost immediately and was extended to the deportees. Ghettos were established in Kaunas, Vilnius, and Šiauliai. Nearly 42,000 Jews were crowded into the Vilnius ghetto; most perished in mass executions in Paneriai (Ponar in Yiddish), a forest outside the city. Kaunas's Ninth Fort was another place of execution. Between June and November 1941 about 200,000 out of an estimated 220,000 Lithuanian Jews were murdered—many of the murders took place over a two-day time span.

Lithuania's Jews had, understandably, preferred Russian occupation to Nazi rule. This situation was exploited by Nazi propaganda and may have influenced the behavior of some Lithuanians during the German occupation. The role of Lithuanian collaborators in the Holocaust is a sensitive subject. It should be stated that there was also resistance to the German occupation, and there were people who risked their own lives to save Jews: 504 Lithuanians are recognized as Righteous Among the Nations for their courage and humanity.

The Second Soviet Occupation
In July 1944 the advancing Red Army reached Lithuania's eastern border. The country was swiftly taken over and, with the agreement of the United States and Britain, the Soviet Union reclaimed it as a Soviet republic. The most oppressive years of the Soviet occupation followed. Over 500,000 Lithuanians were deported, forced into exile, jailed, or shot. Stalinist Russia was a place of seemingly

random violence: purges, tortures, executions, and disappearances. In response to these events, tens of thousands of resistance fighters waged an unsuccessful partisan war against the Soviet regime. The last partisan was killed in combat in 1965.

Stalin's death in 1953 alleviated some of the horror, but the day-to-day lives of many Lithuanians were cloaked in fear and subjugation. As the decades passed, Soviet policies changed from violence to more ideological means of control. The authorities promoted the immigration of non-Lithuanian workers, especially Russians, as a way of integrating Lithuania into the Soviet Union and to encourage industrial development. However, the Lithuanians managed to preserve a sense of national identity throughout this period.

The Restoration of Independence
Most historians view the idea put forward by the Lithuanian press in 1986 of reinstating pre-Soviet street names as the first small step toward independence. Lithuanians gave active support to Mikhail Gorbachev's program of social and political reform, and in 1988 the first official pro-independence movement, Sąjūdis, was formed. A founding member, Vytautas Landsbergis, served as a de facto head of state from March 1990 until the first presidential elections in 1993. In 1989, Sąjūdis was integral in creating the human chain that extended

from Vilnius to Tallinn—nearly two million people held hands over 400 miles (650 km) on the fiftieth anniversary of the Molotov-Ribbentrop Pact in order to draw the world's attention to the fate of the Baltic nations.

On March 11, 1990, the Supreme Council of Lithuania (the future Seimas, or parliament) proclaimed a sovereign Lithuanian state and demanded the withdrawal of Soviet forces. The USSR demanded revocation of the Act and began applying sanctions against Lithuania. Demonstrations erupted on January 13, 1991, when Soviet forces stormed the parliament building in Vilnius along with the television tower. The crowds in front of parliament were able to stop the oncoming tanks, but fourteen people were shot dead when the army seized control of the tower. Not until the failed putsch in Moscow by the Communist Old Guard in August that year was Lithuania finally rid of the Soviets. In 1994 Lithuania joined NATO's Partnership for Peace program and Vilnius's Old Town made it on to UNESCO's World Heritage Sites. Membership in NATO was ratified in 2004.

EU Membership

Lithuania's first steps toward entering the European Union began with the signing of an Association Agreement in June 1995. The state faced two large hurdles: the Ignalina power plant with its Chernobyl-style reactor, and the country's death penalty. The death penalty was abolished in 1998, but the nuclear reactor posed bigger problems as it provided all of the country's energy. Soon after independence Swedish officials had stepped in to update and maintain the reactor, fallout from which would have devastating effects in Scandinavia. Many EU member states argued vehemently that the power plant should be closed in the interests of public safety. The lengthy decommissioning process should end sometime in 2015. In the May 2003 referendum 91 percent of Lithuanians voted to join the EU. On May 1, 2004, Lithuania became an EU member. Many cities celebrated with a fanfare in the belief that this was the beginning of a partnership that would finally be beneficial to their small country.

TYPES OF LITHUANIANS
The Lithuanians divide themselves into distinct groups based on regional stereotypes. A well-known folktale states that the Devil went around Lithuania with a sack, taking a man from each of the four regions. When the Devil reached his destination he put down the sack. The man from Dzūkija was the first to jump out as fear drove his legs to run home. Next to emerge was the man from Suvalkija, who sat and waited until the others got out of the sack so that he could use it himself. He asked the man from Žemaitija why he was still in the bag, to which he responded that if he was put

in the bag then he would wait until he was taken out. Basically, the stereotypes are as follows: people from Žemaitija are quiet, brooding, and not born to action, those from Suvalkija are thrifty, and those from Dzūkija are cowardly. The region of Aukštaitija escapes pigeonholing.

Within the four regions there are smaller ethnic enclaves. Visaginas, home of the Ignalina nuclear power plant, makes an interesting detour. It has wide boulevards reminiscent of Moscow, even though traffic isn't a particular problem. The many ethnic Russians who have grown up in the town speak Lithuanian poorly. As a purely Russian subgroup they have remained uninfluenced by changes outside.

ETHNIC MINORITIES

Lithuania, with its historical influx of visitors, both welcome and unwelcome, has a number of ethnic minorities. Interestingly, the country has integrated more populations into itself than historically have been forced upon it from the outside by invading forces. Vilnius serves as good example; when you are walking through its winding Old Town streets, you will hear the residents speaking Lithuanian, Polish, and Russian.

Outside the capital a few ethnic groups of note include the Karaims (Karaites), Tatars, and Roma. After the battle of Žalgiris (Grünwald) in 1410, the Karaims, brought from the Crimea by Vytautas to fight the Teutonic Knights, settled in the area around Trakai. They are Turkic followers of a sect of Judaism who only believe in the written Law, or *Tanakh*, and who reject all later rabbinical teachings. A small population still lives there to this day. The Tatar population, which is dwindling, survives in a few pockets in the Lukiškės suburb of Vilnius.

Historically, Lithuania's many widely dispersed Jewish communities made a notable contribution to the country's life; about 10,000 survived the Holocaust. By 1998 the Jewish population had fallen to 4,500.

THE JEWISH LEGACY

Lithuania's Jews, in Yiddish *Litvaks*, were famous among their coreligionists for rabbinical scholarship and intellectual rigor. Invited into Lithuania by its pagan rulers in the fourteenth century, they were given significant rights and privileges. During the reign of Gediminas they prospered and were free from persecution, which was not the case in many other parts of Europe. However, after Gediminas's death, depending on the ruler, the Jewish population was either put under scrutiny or left unbothered. They continued to play an important role in the economy and enjoyed a large degree of civic autonomy.

In the eighteenth century there was a flowering of Jewish religious and cultural life. The seminaries of

Vilnius were so famous that it was called the Jerusalem of the North. The most prominent Jewish figure in Lithuania's history is the Gaon of Vilna (Rabbi Elijah ben Judah Solomon Zalman), who lived during the latter half of the 1700s. He strongly opposed Hasidism (Judaism's mystical revivalist movement), was a prolific writer and Talmudic scholar, and fostered a spirit of rational inquiry. With the spread of the Enlightenment, many Lithuanian Jews became devotees of the secular Jewish *Haskala* movement in Eastern Europe, and today there are many leading academics, scientists, and philosophers of Lithuanian Jewish descent.

In 1860, according to the Tsarist census, nearly 56 percent of the population of Vilnius was Jewish. In 1867, and again in 1891, famine, leading to the outbreak of cholera, and pogroms in Southern Russia led to mass emigration to the West. Today there are still strong communities of Jews of Lithuanian descent around the world, especially in Israel, the United States, and South Africa. Despite the drain of emigration, Lithuania remained the heartland of a vibrant modern Yiddish culture.

Although many Jews left the country between 1920 and 1941, the Jewish population of Vilnius remained around 30 percent. When the war began in Poland in 1939 many Polish Jews fled to Vilnius. Of the 77,000 Jews living in Vilnius according to the 1941 census, only 2,000 survived the Holocaust.

Today many people with Litvaks in their family tree visit Lithuania, and specialized tours covering its Jewish history are available. A notable scholar

and local celebrity, Dovid Katz, cofounded the
Vilnius Yiddish Institute, which is part of Vilnius
University. In summer students of all ages attend
the Yiddish language courses that are offered. Katz
himself travels extensively throughout the Baltic to
document the last living native Yiddish speakers.

GOVERNMENT AND POLITICS

Because of the years of Soviet occupation, in which
propaganda and half-truths were par for the course,
most Lithuanians, though ardent nationalists, have
a skeptical outlook on politics and government.
However, this mistrust is tempered by a sort of
practical understanding that it is difficult to get any
work done without getting one's hands a bit dirty.

The Constitution

The Lithuanian constitution was ratified on October
25, 1992. As one would expect, a great deal of
attention is paid to the idea of democracy and
asserting the rights of the republic to defend itself
against any attacks on its sovereignty. Lithuania's
status as an independent democratic republic can
only be revoked by a referendum and a three-
fourths vote by Lithuanian citizens. Constitutional
provisions include free health care for all citizens,
pensions, funds for the unemployed, and aid for
women and children. The Constitution also allows
for religious teaching in public schools on a
discretionary basis.

Parliament

The Lithuanian government is made up of a legislature and the executive, comprised of the president, the prime minister, and his Council of Ministers. (An independent judiciary interprets the Constitution and determines exactly where each branch's jurisdiction lies.) The Seimas, or parliament, has 141 members. Various political parties receive a proportional amount of seventy of the seats, and the remaining seventy-one seats are filled by representatives of single constituencies. Ministers hold office for four years and must be over the age of twenty-five and not concurrently employed or holding another government position. It is the Seimas that approves the prime minister and can force the government's resignation.

The Presidency

The Lithuanian president is elected by the citizens and is the head of state. The president appoints the prime minister with the approval of the Seimas, but can appoint the commander-in-chief of the armed forces on his or her own authority. The office of president is held for five years for no more than two consecutive terms. Candidates must be at least forty years old.

The first president of the republic was Valdas Adamkus, whose family had fled Lithuania during the Second World War. Adamkus spent most of his life in the United States and worked for almost thirty years for the US Environmental Protection Agency. His visits back to Lithuania became more frequent after *perestroika*, and his first term in office began in 1998 and ended in 2003. His successor, former Vilnius mayor Rolandas Paksas, was at the forefront of the first major scandal in the republic when it was revealed that he'd had dealings with Russian "biznizmen"—usually a term reserved for those involved with organized crime— and that the sources of his campaign funding were suspect. Paksas was impeached by a parliamentary vote on April 6, 2004. The 2004 election was won by the then seventy-seven-year-old Adamkus.

Adamkus has had his share of controversy. His Lithuanian passport was issued in 1992 and he was elected in 1998, having lived in the country for the three years required to be a presidential candidate. However, many people believed that although on paper he was resident in Lithuania, he had actually been living in the USA until 1996 or even 1997. In order to show that this was an unfounded rumor Adamkus was featured in a full spread in the daily *Lietuvos Rytas* with an explanation of his past, present, and future commitment to Lithuania.

SLIPPERY BUSINESS

Adamkus invited the press to come and view his apartment in Šiauliai in order to disprove claims by his opponents that he did not in fact reside there. One of the many proofs furnished was the way his slippers (*šlepetės*) were placed next to the bed, and a photograph of this domestic scene was burned into people's minds. Accompanying it came many jokes about the slippers running for the presidency (as they were the true resident of the apartment). The joke survived into the summer of 2006, when the sculptor Jonas Mileris made a monument to slippers on the main street in Šiauliai. As the monument hadn't been officially permitted it was taken down on the day of its erection. And even though Adamkus is well liked, and many Lithuanians understand his possibly having a toe on either side of the Atlantic, jokes remain about slippers being the best type of shoes for a president. Adamkus's advancing age has only added an extra element to the joke's popularity.

ATTITUDES TO THE EUROPEAN UNION

Lithuanians, we have seen, tend to be skeptical when it comes to politics. Polls have been taken regularly since the end of the 1990s and up to the present in order to gauge public attitudes toward EU accession and membership. As a small country with a history of being invaded, subjugated, and marginalized, it is unsurprising that accession was met with some cynicism.

A major issue was the decision to close down the Ignalina power plant. Some Lithuanians viewed this act of compliance as making them junior to the richer Western European nations— and in fact the sentiment is somewhat apropos, rather like boys in a tree house shouting down tasks to another little boy, making him go through a series of hurdles that they themselves never did while dangling the carrot of membership in front of him. After all, France is one of the most nuclear dependent countries in the world— although Ignalina is admittedly a Chernobyl-style reactor, which causes many outside the country to see it only as a potential hazard.

The media have been a major factor in helping the Lithuanians come to see the EU as beneficial. Some social historians consider that at the end of 1998 it was the Lithuanian media that swayed public opinion in favor of joining the EU, through the TV program *Europe Square* and the launch of the weekly "Euro plus" supplement to the daily newspaper *Respublika*.

THE ECONOMY
Lithuania has been rather aggressive, and perhaps more importantly successful, in its move to create a stable economy. The republic's liberal trade

policy has attracted a number of foreign investors, including its Scandinavian neighbors and Russia, and good relations are the norm. The Baltic nations also have a sense of being banded together—primarily by their common history of usurpation by the Russian and Soviet states, but also by the idea that small countries should help each other out. The Lithuanians and Latvians tend to have a warm political relationship, whereas the Estonians are seen as slightly more difficult to understand, which makes sense considering that their language is Finno-Ugric, as opposed to Indo-European, in origin.

chapter two

VALUES & ATTITUDES

LITHUANIAN-NESS

Lithuanians when abroad can usually pick one another out of the crowd, even though physically they are similar to their Latvian and Polish neighbors. Mannerisms and nuanced gestures have a great deal to do with this, but there is a broader sense of shared qualities. There is a firm idea of national character. As with all generalizations these will not hold true for every person, but Lithuanians tend to be tall, with light-colored hair, eyes, and complexion. They have a natural reserve that may at first be misconstrued as shyness or standoffishness, but they are very warm and true once befriended. They are viewed as thinkers with a strain of melancholy and romanticism, whose emotions may be bottled up or discussed in calm terms over a cup of coffee or tea with friends.

Lithuanians when first introduced will often seem quite formal and distant. But once one is accepted into a group, in either a work or a social setting, their warmth is palpable: help is given freely and their communal spirit is evident in their problem-solving skills. There is a reluctance to embarrass others, unless it is to point out that a person is not maintaining social norms.

SELF-CONTAINMENT

To foreigners Lithuanians can sometimes appear devious: they may not answer questions directly, may be evasive about details when pressed, or may seem not always to answer with complete honesty. Some cultural anthropologists suggest that this reluctance to disclose information, especially to outsiders or people they don't know particularly well, is the result of Soviet rule, when indiscretion could land a person in prison. Others are inclined to think that it is a true Lithuanian characteristic. Another theory is that the Lithuanian language itself allows for a level of obliqueness. For example, if one were to hurt one's toe or foot, in English one would say which part of the body was hurt, whereas a Lithuanian would merely say they had hurt their leg, as the need for specificity isn't necessary. When speaking about time, a Lithuanian would describe a six-week period as a month and a half, or an eighteen-month period as a year and a half.

This kind of behavior can be disconcerting, but to regard it as evasive or sneaky is mistaken— Lithuanians in general are apt not to let others know about their problems or issues unless they are close friends. The reason for this is two-fold: specificity is often seen as an unnecessary flourish, and weakness is regarded as something that should be hidden. In the case of the hurt leg versus toe, only when speaking with a medical professional would a Lithuanian go into details. A friend or colleague would not need this information—to offer it would presuppose that they had a great attachment to their own body parts, so much so that only details would make them feel settled about what had occurred. The attitude is that one should not waste anyone's time with unnecessary details, and that specificity is only offered when needed. Furthermore, holding oneself together at all costs is a virtue, and an important part of the national self-image. Emotional outbursts are not well-regarded and people who display a great deal of emotion are ignored or avoided in direct proportion to how outlandish and frequent their outbursts are.

EMOTIONALISM AND MYSTICISM
That being said, sentimentality and melancholy are also national traits. Lithuanians, especially after drinking alcohol, enjoy soul-searching. Specific types of emotional displays are considered normal, if not entirely appropriate. For example, when Vytautas Landsbergis, who had been the de facto head of state, gave an impassioned speech in Brussels after the former Communist leader Brazauskas won the 1993 presidential elections, his emotions were seen as the grief of the nation. To complicate matters further, another national characteristic is

Schadenfreude, the enjoyment of another's misfortune. The Lithuanian version carries a bit more pathos, as *piktdžiuga* is a compound word created by the terms "angry" and "joy" and is specific to the feeling of being consoled by the fact that your enemy or a person disliked by you has had an unfortunate event in their life.

The national character embraces swings between poles. Lithuanians will complain, be intolerant, envious, and willfully ignorant, and simultaneously be open-minded, loyal to those whose beliefs they do not accept, and revel in romantic idealism and sentimentalism. A mysticism that is not often seen in Western culture pervades the Lithuanian consciousness. There is an idea of largesse, or generosity of spirit, that allows an individual to contain a multiplicity of different emotions and personas, and sometimes even duplicity.

This can also feed into paranoid thinking. Many older adults still at least partially believe that the KGB or similar such agencies control the government, dominate political life, and are very much interested in what they as individuals are doing. But within this slide of the continuum one thing is constant—Lithuanians are generally sincere in the majority of their words and actions.

LOVE OF NATURE

Feeding their romantic idealism and mysticism is a strong connection with the natural world; almost all

Lithuanians have a deep and abiding love of nature. The countryside is viewed as the place where one can return to a simpler existence, and the landscape can startle a person back into understanding what is most important in life. The natural world strips life down to the essential functions of eating, sleeping, socializing, and getting in tune with one's true self.

Plucked from Obscurity

The employees of an international corporation were being taken on a morale-building excursion to the lakes in summer. On the way the foreigners in the bus were surprised to see their Lithuanian colleagues drinking beer so early in the morning. In the course of the journey some rather boisterous passengers demanded a pit stop, and the driver obliged by pulling off the side of the road. As people returned from relieving themselves in the woods, the foreigners were further surprised by the Lithuanian women— some of whom were high up on the company ladder—who after a while came back with mushrooms they had picked to supplement the picnic. Although city career women, they still knew which mushrooms could be eaten and which not, without consulting a book. Their Lithuanian fellow passengers hooted and hollered their approval of the bounty, despite the holdup it had caused. It seemed that the party had truly begun now that a traditional, natural element had been introduced into the proceedings.

Most Lithuanian city dwellers have a family or friends' country house where they go to live a simple and relaxing life for a few weeks every year. Even people raised in cities can usually name the different species of trees and flowers, but perhaps most extraordinary is their ability to find mushrooms and pick them during any sort of outing. They are fastidious in their care for nature and will leave a picnic area exactly as they found it, taking all their trash away with them.

MOBILITY: MOVING OUT AND ON

Lithuanians in small villages live at a subsistence level. Most young people with initiative or a desire for more leave their hometown and move to a nearby city to further their education. Young Lithuanians are for the most part very ambitious, which has resulted in the creation of a highly educated group of people and also a great number of émigrés. There has recently been a brain drain, as young professionals opt to leave the country for higher Western salaries. In recent years London, Dublin, and to a lesser extent Chicago have received many of these émigrés. In Lithuania real estate prices have gone up in recent years, so many professionals move abroad for a higher salary and then return home with enough money to purchase the house that they could not have afforded on a Lithuanian salary. Several think tanks and conferences have been convened to stop the brain drain, but little has been done to give incentives to young professionals to stay in the country. Also, as the population becomes more educated many low-level jobs are left without enough people to fill them.

PATRIOTISM: FROM THE BALTIC TO THE BLACK SEA

If you tipple with Lithuanian men for longer than an hour and ask what the greatest feat of the nation has been you will at first hear about basketball—the country's greatest players, which ones went to which American NBA team, and how the Lithuanians will win the next Olympic games. This will be followed, if enough alcohol is consumed, by an account of the Lithuanian empire's extension from the Baltic to the Black

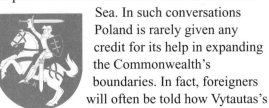 Sea. In such conversations Poland is rarely given any credit for its help in expanding the Commonwealth's boundaries. In fact, foreigners will often be told how Vytautas's horse drank water from the Black Sea. Pointing out that horses are disinclined to drink salt water will be met by dubious stares and usually a retelling of the story. In fact, this story is told partially tongue-in-cheek, and many Lithuanians can laugh at themselves, but foreigners should refrain from commenting on their history or politics.

Team Spirit
In the 2004 Olympics the Lithuanian
basketball team came in fourth place. During
the qualifying games people crowded on to
the streets in the major Lithuanian cities,
waving flags, toasting each other with beers,
and hugging one another. When the team lost,
and it was understood they were no longer
Olympic hopefuls this time round, the crowds
took to the streets again, waving flags and
making merry, and chanted, just as ardently,
"We almost won."

RULES ARE MEANT TO BE BROKEN

Lithuanians feel a sense of pride when they see
that one of their own has figured out a new way
to bend a rule. An exceptionally wide grin is
reserved for those who have managed to follow
the letter of the law but subvert its spirit. Many
Lithuanians follow the principle of finding the
path of least resistance, and always look for the
easiest way to navigate through problems or
issues caused by rules. Lithuanians possess a
talent for spotting a weakness in bureaucracy and
using it to their advantage. Some think that this
ability developed under the Soviets, when an
individual's cleverness was essential for survival
and any opportunity to undermine the system was
taken. However, this behavior still persists in

today's democracy, which leads many to wonder if it isn't in fact evidence of something else, such as national character. Generally rules are seen as guidelines or signposts, outside which one may walk, if briskly and without too much fanfare.

BRIBERY, CORRUPTION, AND CANDIES

High-level corruption is found in the Lithuanian political world. And although most scandals manage to disappear rather quickly from the public eye, day-to-day life mimics the bigger political arena. Everything in Lithuania moves faster with alcohol, chocolates, or flowers. The giving of these is never described as a bribe. Instead the attitude is that the gift is a measure of good faith that a person will do their best to help you. Gifts tend to not be lavish, just small tokens such as a bouquet of flowers or a bottle of alcohol. The unspoken consensus is that anything costing less than 125 Lt cannot be considered a bribe, but is just a gift.

Many foreigners are frustrated by the way civil servants especially need to be coerced into doing their jobs by a simple gift; however, these small tokens are an important part of daily life. Most foreigners will not have to grease too many wheels, but Lithuanians have to make donations or give gifts in many circumstances, including to doctors during hospitalization in order to receive better than rudimentary health care.

Going to the Dogs

A member of parliament was found to have used a government car and driver to pick up his dog and take it for a walk. When it was revealed that he was misusing his office and government property, his response was that the government car—unlike his own—was shabby, and for that reason should be used to transport his pet.

GENDER

Many women are as well educated as their husbands, if not more so. In the large cities it is not uncommon for men in blue-collar jobs, such as construction or carpentry, to have wives who work in offices. (An interesting holdover from Soviet times is that middle-aged and older women can be found in the construction industry doing work such as painting.) A very definite machismo informs many social interactions between men and women, but the relationship is nuanced. Foreigners often see Lithuanian women as compliant and even subservient. In most instances these inequalities are more for show: many women feel that there is a need to allow a man to have his dignity, and so men are treated with deference in public. However, this imbalance is often righted in private.

A Man's Voice

Before EU accession, a Lithuanian Airlines flight from London to Vilnius was full of young men who had been turned away from the UK. They had claimed to be coming as tourists but were found to be carrying the tools of various blue-collar trades, so the British authorities sent them home. Once on the plane the boys proceeded to demand alcohol and smoke in the lavatories. None of the stewardesses was able to get them to calm down. Finally a pilot emerged and quietly told them to settle down, which they did. When an American on the flight told the story to a Lithuanian friend her response was, "A man's voice is a man's voice," explaining why the boys had listened.

Foreign men are often impressed by Baltic women, who are in general good-looking, slender, and well dressed. In the large cities even a woman of little means will look her best when stepping out to shop for a few sundries. In winter snow and slush the women manage to keep their boots shiny and their coat hems clean. Outside appearance is very important in how a woman is regarded. (Men are not held to such high aesthetic standards.) Staying slim, for women, is an important part of the culture, and it is not uncommon to see a couple out dining with the man eating a large plate of rich food and the woman having a small salad or coffee. At dinner parties or in restaurants you will often see groups of friends and couples where the men sit on one side of the table and the women on the other, with both groups involved in two distinct conversations. The younger generations tend to be more integrated on social occasions.

Fur-ious: A Woman's Voice

An American woman who had been living in Vilnius for many years was walking down the street one wintry morning when a big car sped past, spraying her with slush. Upset as she felt, she became really angry when she realized that another woman in a beautiful fur coat had been drenched too—and that her response was a look of defeat. The American walked up to the man in his car as he waited at a stoplight, knocked on his window, and began to explain in her best Lithuanian how piggish his behavior was, pointing out the fur coat, now filthy and caked in slush. Shocked by the screaming American and the sight of the Lithuanian woman in her ruined coat, the large man in his Mercedes began to apologize immediately. He parked his car and instantly offered to pay the dry-cleaning bill for both women.

Even in this rather macho society, chivalry is important, but most Lithuanian women almost never insist upon it. Additionally, foreign women who are outspoken will more often be listened to than their Lithuanian counterparts.

ATTITUDES TOWARD FOREIGNERS

Foreigners are treated at once like idiots and kings. Lithuanians will go out of their way to be nice and hospitable to foreign guests, but will also mock their stupidity at any opportunity. The reasons for this are slightly complicated, but basically boil down to a mixture of envy and resentment stemming from a perceived imbalance in what foreigners have and what Lithuanians have; it is assumed that all foreigners always have a higher standard of living than Lithuanians. Also there is a slight resentment of the opportunities that Western foreigners are allowed, which many Lithuanians feel they are not. These relate to economic advantages and the ability not have to suffer discomfitures, such as when trying to secure visas to travel to the USA or other countries. However, foreigners are also seen as rather spoiled and unable to deal with hardships, and so regarded as naive children in a world full of adults who have faced great challenges.

Being foreign in Lithuania gives one license to do many silly things; however, as more foreigners enter the country the blind eye to shenanigans is lessening. Lithuania has become a destination in the last few years for stag parties from the UK and other parts of Western Europe. Most Lithuanians do not have a particular aversion to this sort of tourism and view it as an inevitable part of economic growth. It is a source of revenue, but it has changed the physical face of Vilnius's nightlife—some say for the worse. Tourists waving around large amounts of cash and showing little savvy are often the targets of petty crime.

Nonwhite foreigners will have a hard time blending in and will be met with both outright racism and fascination. The larger cities will be more welcoming, whereas even a white Lithuanian-American whose language skills are quite good will be met with suspicion in smaller villages. When visiting smaller towns and villages, the foreigner will often be "shouted at" in whichever foreign language the person knows, so English speakers may encounter an older Lithuanian woman yelling at them in broken German. The loud talk is merely an attempt to make you understand, in the same way an American might speak English slowly to a newly arrived immigrant. And for many villagers, foreigners are just that—foreigners—and therefore any foreign tongue should be comprehensible. It is not really hostile, just the same sort of cluelessness that causes Americans to use their high-school Spanish in Italy. Take it as a lesson on how to treat foreigners in your own country.

Those raised in the USA will find that a surefire way to draw attention to oneself is to set out for a jog. Exercise in this part of the world is strictly indoors, and people out for a run will often be laughed at, or even taunted.

Independent Thoughts

A group of American residents in Vilnius decided to have a barbecue in their communal courtyard to celebrate the Fourth of July. The area was quite large and exposed on two sides to the street. An older Lithuanian woman, a resident busybody, came out to complain that the barbecue was filling the air with smoke and that this was a pollution of her environment, even though she lived far from where the smoke was rising. She was quite angry and said that in her fifty years in the building no one had ever had a barbecue, and now foreigners were coming in and having one. When one of the Americans explained politely that it was their independence day, and that she had celebrated all four Lithuanian independence days, she relented and ceased her tirade. They had managed to change her rather conservative views of what should occur in a courtyard.

CLASS AND MONEY

Showing off is considered tasteless. That said, everyone with something to show off usually does. Lithuanians have a special disdain for "New Russians" or "New Lithuanians," who advertise their wealth by purchasing upscale vehicles and wearing expensive but flashy clothing. The republic is still small enough for many, men for the most part, to go for the status symbol of a foreign car not for sale in the country, so that they can boast of having the only model in the land. Also vacations and holidays have become markers of the wealthy, and sitting on a beach is considered *de rigueur*. Many rich Lithuanians now opt for adventure travel to exotic destinations. Again, status is achieved by showing where one has been, knowing that few of one's compatriots have been to the same destination.

An ever-widening chasm is growing between the lower and upper classes, leaving those in the middle leaping for either end. Money and financial matters will not often be discussed up front, but be aware that as a foreigner what might be an inexpensive meal for you could be quite pricey for the average Lithuanian. When dining in a group, don't embarrass your Lithuanian friends by choosing an expensive venue or by offering to pay for their meal. If you are dining *à deux*, however, and you are a man and your companion is a woman, it will be expected.

RELIGION

As with many things Lithuanian, the attitude toward religion is at once what it is and its exact opposite. The country is predominantly Roman Catholic and a distinctly Catholic sensibility seems to inform both art and home décor. In fact, a few rather Catholic thoughts do permeate society, such as the idea of being part of a larger scheme of things. Thus Lithuanians are quite communal and help one another out. The concept of humility is also quite important; braggarts are not well regarded.

Churches tend to be filled on Sundays; while most Lithuanians consider Polish people to be slightly fanatical in their devotion, they are not as agnostic as their Scandinavian neighbors. Older Lithuanians tend to be truly religious. But even this devout group is not above suspicion, as in Lithuania churches are makeshift senior centers where the elderly come to gossip and have a chance to socialize after Mass with their peers. An old saying states that Lithuanians are Catholics on Sunday, pagans during the workweek, and simply drunk on Saturdays.

Setting aside the reasons people may have for attending services, it is true to say that the national character is informed by a religious spirit. Lithuanians when watching political scandals unfold are apt first to chastise the wrongdoer and then to soften their blows; there is a firm belief in the possibility of redemption—and that no situation is completely unfixable by one's own actions. Of course only after an act of contrition is made and penance is shown will the public re-embrace its fallen leaders. This sort of scheduled tolerance is an interesting snapshot of the culture at large as it points to a kind of optimism that is not so easily seen in daily interactions, where conversations about the hardships of life are common.

Vilnius, we have seen, was once considered the Jerusalem of the North. Of the many synagogues before the Second World War only one remains; the script above its doorway reads "For my house is a house of prayer that calls to all the nations." The tolerance shown toward other religions, although historically true, was significantly marred by the actions of some

Lithuanians during the Second World War. Today in Lithuania very few religions other than Catholicism have a strong following, but the culture is one of tolerance, with the stipulation that no religion, or government for that matter, should be allowed to force any sort of ideology upon the people as a whole.

Churches

A visitor newly arrived in Lithuania had broken the heel of her shoe while walking through the Old Town of Vilnius. She stopped in a shoe shop where she was told that the repair could not be carried out at that location but in another shop just down the street across from the church. The woman thanked the shopkeeper politely for explaining very slowly and carefully exactly how to get to the other store. It was only upon leaving the shop that she realized that to her left and to her right and directly in front of her were three churches.

SUPERSTITION

A certain fervor, not found in the celebration of either pagan or Catholic traditions, can be seen in the way many people adhere to the rules for not bringing bad luck upon oneself or others. Feigning spitting over one's shoulder to ward off bad luck is quite common. Other customs include, when telling a white lie, not to say that someone is sick, as this could tempt fate and actually cause them to fall ill. The superstitions are mostly observed as a preventative measure and are done "just in case," to insure that one's actions do not cause unwanted results, although it is not firmly believed that they, in fact, will.

Set into the ground on Cathedral Square in Vilnius is a pavement tile that is marked *stebuklas*, or miracle. Some believe that it marks the starting point of the two-million person human chain that linked Vilnius with Tallinn on August 23, 1989. These people are mistaken. Even the sculptor who made the tile insisted it was for fun, but the legend has become widely believed in the country, feeding into the vein of romantic nationalism. Others believe that this is a spot where, if one makes a wish and turns in a circle, the wish—if kept secret—will be granted, and that bad luck will befall anyone who gives the exact coordinates of the tile. No one has managed to disprove either notion conclusively.

chapter three

FESTIVALS & CUSTOMS

HOLIDAYS

In a place where it can snow for half the year and rain can fall on the parade of summer, festivals and holidays become important ways to brighten peoples' mood. Official state holidays mean a day off from work. Most Lithuanians enjoy a paid four- to six-week holiday every year. As summer temperatures can fluctuate, many people simply take a week or more when the weather begins to warm up. During a heat wave some companies will leave just a few souls behind to man the phones and keep things ticking over—every one else will be at a summerhouse, preferably near a lake or the Baltic Sea.

Since Lithuania was one of the last European countries to convert to Christianity many of its Christian festivals have a distinctly pagan flavor. Below is a list of official holidays, when government offices and banks are closed. Other holidays that are always celebrated, some of whose dates change yearly, are the major Christian holidays in the Gregorian calendar. The two most important are Easter weekend and the Feast of the Assumption. The first Sunday in May

is Mother's Day. Expect shorter working hours
for businesses on Christmas Eve and Easter.

January 1 New Year's Day
February 16 Independence Day
March 11 Restoration of Independence Day
May 1 Day of the Workers
June 24 St. John's Day (Midsummer)
July 6 Lithuanian Statehood (Crowning of Mindaugas)
August 15 Feast of the Assumption
November 1-2 All Souls' Day
December 25–26 Christmas

New Year's Eve and New Year's Day
The celebration of New Year's Eve in
Lithuania is similar to other parts of the
world, and includes firework displays
and the drinking of champagne. The
following day, even though many
may still be feeling the effects of the
previous night's overindulgence, there is
a variety of events to celebrate the start of the
year and new beginnings.

In Vilnius, older well-heeled citizens spend the
evening watching *La Traviata* at the Opera
House, followed by dinner in one of the city's
classier establishments. Masquerade parties are
becoming more popular in the country, especially
with the younger generation. Many attend the
fireworks display along the northern banks of the
Neris River, which is visible from Cathedral
Square; the boisterous festivities see champagne

corks flying through the air and a convivial spirit taking over the crowd. Amateur pyrotechnics and midnight kissing skills are sometimes shown off—both of which can be a bit dangerous. For those staying at home there are TV programs known for being stretched out and rather silly, with Lithuanian talent presiding.

New Year's Day usually is spent visiting friends and enjoying food. The making of New Year's resolutions, newly conformed to on the morning of January 1, is also typical. In Vilnius families often stop by for one last look at the city's Christmas trees—either on Cathedral Square or Town Square. Typical of Lithuanians, an element of whimsy is usually added to the Christmas celebration. For example, one year the tree was made with an opening and extension so that people could enter it.

Independence Day: February 16
Independence Day is celebrated with vigor by some, while others are just happy to enjoy the day off work. Expect to see the flag waving in a few more places than usual, and the requisite fireworks display. Concerts take place in Vilnius on Cathedral Square, and a there is small parade near the President's Palace. The president also throws a lavish party for the city's elite, and the media coverage of it is avidly read the following day to see which celebrities and people of note were there—and what they wore.

Shrovetide

The celebration of Shrovetide, or *Užgavėnės*,
takes place before the austerity of Lent begins.
Traditionally the largest fair is in Vilnius, where
townsfolk dress up in the costumes of characters
from folklore or as particular stereotypes. For
example, being a policeman is okay, but no one
would dress up as a specific police officer. In the
original pagan tradition all the masks depicted
animals, such as goats,
bears, or storks. Later the
idea of representing types
of people came in, often
with strong social
overtones as people
dressed up as members of
minority groups such as

the Roma, Jews, or Protestants. These less than
politically correct customs have now morphed
into more innocuous forms, with costumes
representing shady doctors or bribe-loving police
officers. Some believe that with the beginning of
winter this celebration helped to express, and
exorcise, those forces that brought fear to people.
In pagan times wild animals were not only
dangerous in a very real sense, but in animist
belief contained a spiritual power too. Later,
society's scapegoats were what instilled fear and
were paraded in the festival.

Užgavėnės involves excess and abundance.
Pancakes are integral to this. In Vilnius's Town

Hall Square large fires and frying pans work to create a meter-long pancake every year. The idea is to eat and drink to your heart's content before the Lenten fast that begins the following day. Some scheduled entertainment also occurs, including a large female effigy made of straw to symbolize winter. Later she is burned to show its demise. A fight is held between a large man, Lašininis, and a puny one, Kanapinis. Not to ruin the end, but the latter, symbolizing short days and lack of food in winter, always loses.

St. Casimir's Day

St. Casimir's Day, on March 4, is celebrated with a great flourish as he is the patron saint of Lithuania. On the weekend closest to St. Casimir's Day, a fair called "Kaziukas" takes

place in most major towns, but the largest is held in Vilnius's Old Town. Folk artists hawk their wares alongside food vendors selling sweet snacks. The festive specialty is *verbos*, a collection of dried flowers, grasses, and herbs, tied together into a long stick. With both color, courtesy of the flowers, and a nice aroma from the herbs, the sticks decorate homes for the duration of Lent and are later used on Palm Sunday—as observably palm trees are scarce in these parts.

Easter Sunday and Monday

The most important holiday in the Christian calendar, Easter falls on the first Sunday of spring with a full moon, with a vigil taking place the evening before. The devout fill the churches, together with their less pious brethren who take this opportunity to make amends for less than Christian behavior in previous months. But everyone seems to enjoy the overindulgence of Easter Sunday. So much so that the following Monday is a holiday that most use to recuperate, while others continue to celebrate.

The decorating of eggs to celebrate spring goes back to pagan times. During the Sunday feasting a game is played where people pick their "lucky" hand-painted (hard-boiled) Easter egg. Having chosen an egg, the person challenges others to see whose egg will crack when they strike one against the other. The hope is that your egg will vanquish all others. The game is a great equalizer as all ages play with each other and a lot of discussion is generated around tables about egg-striking strategies; the atmosphere is one of silliness and competitive conviviality.

Since many large Lithuanian cities have a Russian population, the Orthodox Easter celebrations are also notable. Like the Catholic service, the Orthodox service takes place in the evening; however, at midnight there is a procession around the church, with many of the icons being carried around the outside perimeter by parishioners.

All Souls' Day

Halloween has a following among bar and club owners as a way to get people packed in to their establishments, but hasn't quite hit the mainstream yet. A night out on October 31 in any large city promises only a few souls dressed in costume. A distinctly Lithuanian holiday occurs on November 1–2 when the Christian All Souls' Day is intertwined with *Vėlinės*, a pagan holiday commemorating the dead. All Souls' Day is a national holiday and many take the opportunity to visit the graves of relatives to light candles and pray for their souls. In Vilnius at Rasų cemetery a huge bonfire is lit. Marshal Józef Piłsudski's heart—at his request—is interred in his mother's grave in the cemetery. Ethnic Poles who are Lithuanian citizens gather around the bonfire to remember their hero, in what for many Lithuanians is an unwelcome demonstration.

Midsummer and St. John's Day

One of the most vibrant and enjoyable holidays of the year takes place as summer is getting into its swing. And like most Lithuanian holidays, there is both a pagan and a Christian element to it. The Feast of St. John, *Joninės*, is celebrated on June 24, but the evening before is Midsummer, *Rasos*, a very pagan holiday celebrating the shortest night of the year. Many Lithuanians descend on the mounds at Kernavė, a small village about 15 miles (24 km) north of Vilnius, which many believe was the first real settlement of the Baltic tribes. The area is not just archaeologically rich, but historically and socially rich too.

Besides a banquet of food and beer, the highlight of the evening is a two-fold display of what would have been "fireworks" for the ancient pagans: both candles and bonfires. Girls wear wreaths of plants, including medicinal herbs, which later are taken off and sent down the nearby Neris River bearing lit candles. The five mounds of Kernavė provide picture-perfect vantage points to see hundreds of candles slowly burning out as they meander down the river. The surrounding forest adds an element of the surreal as the evening's darkness is punctuated by small candles drifting past, and also a large bonfire. Men and boys jump over the flames of the bonfire in a bid to show off their strength. As alcohol consumption is encouraged on such a night, the results of the bonfire leaps can be anything from comical to mildly disastrous.

On this night it is said that a special fern blossoms in the forest for a moment at midnight. In pagan times boys and girls were encouraged to pair off and look for this blossom, as this was a celebration of fertility. Today's festivities see fewer supporters of the tradition, although sometimes boys find themselves newly attached to ancient beliefs after a few beers. The party in any event lasts the entire night. For a foreigner it is quite a spectacle, especially as the normally reserved Lithuanians will be at their most jolly, and the spirit is catching. Some might even say that the holiday works as a metaphor for the people and the land itself—although seemingly inhospitable on occasion, and perhaps a bit dark, a very real energy and growth coinciding with a sense of possibility lies underneath the surface, and once unveiled commands your attention.

Crowning of Mindaugas

Lithuania's only one true king is celebrated on July 6 with the Coronation of King Mindaugas Day. As with many national celebrations, their sense of patriotism determines how Lithuanians view the holiday, with some people enjoying the break from work and others raising the national flag and commenting on the past glory of Lithuania. Most large cities mark the occasion, but the small town of Kernavė also hosts a small but festive celebration.

Feast of the Assumption

August 15 is *Žolinė*, or the Feast of the Assumption, celebrating the Virgin Mary's ascension to Heaven at the end of her life. This day is a public holiday. There are many small activities throughout town, and the Rumšiškės open-air ethnography museum hosts an event that includes various races and competitions relating to farming or animal husbandry.

Christmas

Most towns and cities have a Christmas tree decorating the main square. In Vilnius's Cathedral Square there is a tree-lighting ceremony watched by many. The holiday is spent with family members and a large meal is prepared by the women. Unlike the roast turkey or goose so popular in Western Europe, in Lithuania the Christmas dish is carp. Traditionally the fish was purchased from the supermarket alive and swimming in a bag of water. Once home it was placed in a tub for safekeeping and occasionally became a family pet for a few hours. Now new EU regulations have been passed that do not allow Lithuanians to buy live carp; instead shopgirls take the selected fish behind a curtain where they do the killing. Many Lithuanians are quite angry about the change.

SPECIAL EVENTS

Lithuanians will take almost any occurrence and turn it into a reason to celebrate. For this reason there are many more holidays and celebrations than the official ones.

Flagging Holidays

On April 19, 1918, the Council of Lithuania adopted the yellow, green, and red bars of the national flag. Not only are the colors common to Lithuanian folk art, but the yellow represents the land's golden hue, green represents nature, and red the blood shed in defending Lithuania. In November of that year the flag was first officially raised in public, but it was banned during the Soviet occupation. On October 7, 1988, the flag was raised on top of Vilnius's Gediminas Castle, where one still waves today.

With their history of being overshadowed or conquered by larger neighbors, Lithuanians, even when not given the day off work, will often commemorate important historical dates by putting out the national flag. The following are the days when many houses or apartment buildings will be festooned with flags.

January 13	Defenders of Freedom
June 14	Day of Mourning and Hope
August 23	Black Ribbon Day (Molotov-Ribbentrop signing)
September 8	Crowning of Vytautas the Great
October 25	Constitution Day

Song Festival

The pan-Baltic festival, which includes the Lithuanian Song Festival, takes place every four years during the first week of July. The next ones will occur in 2011. The gathering sees hundreds of thousands of Lithuanians meeting in Vilnius to perform national folk songs dressed in national costume. The festival is an important means of insuring that young people are made aware of their traditions and learn how to keep them alive.

Vilnius City Festivals
Vilnius plays host to innumerable small festivals, especially in summer and early fall. The main ones are May's International Folklore Festival, which concentrates on music; June's Vilnius Festival, a celebration of classical music; and July's St. Christopher Festival, a large music festival that takes place in various venues throughout the city. In September both the Vilnius City Festival with its fireworks and carnivals and the Vilnius Jazz Festival liven up the capital. Late September's Old Music Festival, featuring medieval and Baroque church music, takes place in churches throughout the city.

chapter four

MAKING FRIENDS

In Lithuania friendship is a far more serious relationship than in other parts of the world. It is a close and lasting bond that is not easily broken. A true friend in Lithuania will come to your house at the drop of a hat to help you talk over a problem, or look after your children for an entire evening so that you can attend a party. Basically they will be a part of your social network and help to make your life easier and simpler. For foreigners making friends in Lithuania is relatively simple. Lithuanians often have large social networks of schoolmates, colleagues, and people whom they have met through mutual acquaintances. Generally speaking, they are interested in meeting foreigners and getting to know their views on life.

MEETING PEOPLE

Foreigners are still seen by many Lithuanians as something of a novelty, so being friendly and striking up conversations in bars and restaurants can be a good way to meet people. You will be considered interesting unless your conversation proves otherwise. Foreigners planning on staying in Lithuania for a while should try to accept all invitations extended to them. If you are unable to make a particular event, reschedule it as Lithuanians tend not to repeat invitations more than once or twice if they are turned down. Also Lithuanians tend to be shy about striking up conversations, but will immerse themselves in one if another person initiates it. Be friendly and you will usually be rewarded. If you make a new acquaintance in this way and exchange phone numbers then calling within a few days to try to meet up again is considered normal.

Many foreigners in Lithuania make the mistake of spending a great deal of their time socializing with other expatriates. As Lithuanian friendships usually take a while to cultivate, foreigners who visit the country for a few months may feel that making friends is difficult. In fact it just requires a bit more effort on their part to spend time with Lithuanian acquaintances.

ACQUAINTANCES

Lithuanians do not refer to people they know as friends unless they feel exceptionally close to them. In fact an acquaintance is referred to as *pažįstamas*, meaning somebody whom you know. A *geras pažįstamas*, or good acquaintance, is someone whom you know well, but is still not considered a friend. To many foreigners it may seem as if Lithuanians put up some proverbial blockades to close friendships. This is in fact true, but once accepted by a Lithuanian the friendship is usually lifelong.

Impertinent Information

An American who had lived in Vilnius for some months was always surprised to find, when running into acquaintances on the streets, that his greeting would be returned by "*Labas, kur eini*?"—"Hello, and where are you off to now?" He finally asked a Lithuanian friend why everyone was so nosy about his whereabouts. The friend explained that the response was similar to being asked "How are you doing?" in English, and that a strictly truthful answer was never really anticipated. The Lithuanians did not expect to be given any truly personal information as they themselves would never freely give it out.

FRIENDS

You will know when someone has truly befriended you because you will brought into their life in a very real way. Lithuanian friends will stop by your residence without calling, will call late at night just to talk, and will help you in every way they can. They are very conscientious and will often go out of their way to help. The exterior, which for so many foreigners is hard to penetrate, is very much a cocoon once you are inside a friendship with a Lithuanian. Even after long separations you will be met without any stiffness. Friendships endure.

Individuals are accepted as being complex and multifaceted, and subjects such as extramarital affairs, which would be taboo in other parts of the world, are discussed openly among friends. Lithuanians can often border on what some Western Europeans and Americans would consider outright abusiveness in close friendships. For example, calling someone "an idiot" for having done something mildly stupid is not considered rude. It also does not mean that the speaker believes they have a low IQ; instead it is pointing out their mistake so that they will not err in the same way again.

Lithuanians, due to their mysticism and natural love of philosophy, often establish friendships through long discussions. It is rare to become true friends with a Lithuanian until you have sorted out some important matters, such as your philosophy of life or your ideas on spirituality. Foreign men will often be "baptized" into a friendship in an evening of heavy drinking, during which one's philosophy, basketball, and women will be discussed with equal fervor. Letting people see how your behavior is changed by alcohol, while proving that you still enjoy each other's company in this altered state, paves the way toward friendship.

INITIAL MEETINGS

Lithuanians generally appear a bit standoffish to American or British foreigners. Usually this is because they are somewhat mistrustful of foreigners and sometimes afraid of being judged by them. They tend to be polite, though, and will use formal forms of address until you invite them to use your first name. If someone is your elder or a business associate who is higher up on the company ladder, then you should wait for them to initiate informal forms of address.

When first meeting someone in a social situation, handshakes are not the norm, as they are on business occasions. They happen most often between men. When a hand is extended to a woman a vigorous handshake is not anticipated. More commonly a nod of the head acts as a greeting, followed by "*Labai malonu*," which means "Pleased to meet you." If during a social function you manage to have a conversation that goes beyond general pleasantries, then a half hug where bodies touch briefly will occur when saying good-bye between members of the opposite sex. In the case of two women, both cheeks will be kissed lightly.

When navigating through social situations it is important to know some rules. Much of American or British small talk is considered prattling. Americans can seem exaggerated to Lithuanians in their use of pleasantries or polite conditionals, such as asking for favors with a great fanfare about not wanting to put a person out. Many Lithuanians will assume a certain insincerity is at work when told to "have a nice day" and the like. Also asking a person "if it isn't too much trouble" before asking a favor, however small, sounds slightly ludicrous when translated. Lithuanians manage to straddle many lines while conversing: they are polite and direct but not aggressive or prying. Thus, asking specific details about a new acquaintance's life is considered rude in social situations. Lithuanians value politeness. If someone sneezes it is considered very rude not to say something along the lines of "Bless you."

Most Lithuanians will try to ascertain your status in life in very brief snippets of a conversation without asking direct questions. Follow their lead. Also, if at any point you falter in a conversation or break a social norm—say by asking a very personal question, such as why a person is not married, or does not have children after having been married for a number of years—you will normally be given cues: the other person may change the subject, break away from the conversation, or give you the pat answer "*Na, toks gyvenimas*," which translates as "Well, such is life." It seems a great deal of energy is invested in ignoring or shunning "bad" behavior, and never being confrontational. The only times directness will occur is in speaking with close friends or when women are dealing with flirtatious men. For the most part, Lithuanian men are sexually direct toward women, in words and sometimes in actions, often making sure their expectations are understood to the detail.

BEING A GUEST

If a Lithuanian invites you to a social event or to participate in an activity with them, the level of their interest in securing your friendship is directly proportional to the type of occasion or activity. The first level is an invitation for coffee. Chats over coffee can span several hours, so if you accept such an invitation it is best to not have booked other engagements soon after. Daytime coffee chats can extend into snacking. Cafés in the large cities are usually full of people sitting about for hours. Lithuanians tend not to eat out very often—so an invitation to dine in an establishment goes beyond the American version of asking someone if they would like to "grab dinner somewhere." It is a more serious invitation. When asking a Lithuanian if they would like to join you for dinner make certain that you pick a reasonably priced place—by Lithuanian standards. If you are male and asking a female she will expect you to pay for her meal.

Invitations Home

If you are invited to a Lithuanian's home then you are most certainly an important business contact or someone who is—or is becoming—a close friend. When entering the house do not under any circumstances shake hands over the threshold—it is considered bad luck. Many Lithuanians wear slippers in the home, so make sure that your socks are in good condition. Also, in winter try to clean off your boots before entering. Be sure to bring your hosts a gift. Flowers, chocolates, and alcohol are best. Whereas in other parts of the world a bottle of wine is the norm, and Lithuanians will cheerily accept it, they themselves are more likely to bring spirits, or champagne for special occasions. Chocolates are always a safe bet, especially if you do not know the lady of the house. The most important thing is to not arrive empty-handed and not to bring Lithuanian products. As a foreigner it is expected that you will bring something more interesting. Your hosts will have probably spent hours preparing your meal and so bringing a good bottle of alcohol or imported chocolates shows proper consideration for their efforts.

For the most part these meals last several hours and involve serious amounts of alcohol. Your host will almost certainly keep your glass topped up and your plate full. In order not to overindulge, it is best to eat and drink slowly. The exception should be when a person makes a toast. The word for "good health" or "cheers" is *Į sveikatą!* Usually the host will be the first to say a few words about how glorious it is to be surrounded by friends, family, and food; your job as a guest is to nod in approval and down everything in your glass if you are having shots. Not doing so will be seen as rude, especially if you are a man. Women are allowed a bit more leeway. At some point in the evening if you are the guest of honor you should make a toast thanking your host or hostess for their hospitality. Give succinct but detailed compliments.

In fact, you will notice that there is a great deal of discussion and that eating seems to be a secondary activity. It is not uncommon to be served cold food, such as cured meats, cheeses, and breads, at the beginning of the meal, followed by something hot, soup or a meat dish, many hours later. As a foreign visitor you should try a bit of everything. Food allergies aren't accepted as valid reasons for not eating particular types of food. Vegetarians may have an especially hard time and if possible should let their host know before the party that they do not eat meat. Even this may sometimes have the host serving a vegetarian a piece of chicken—as it is not meat in some sense. Try to be as gracious as possible.

Picnics

An interim stage in becoming a friend is to be invited to a picnic in summer. These often last many hours, and sometimes take place by a swimming hole. At such events, it would be very uncommon not to have some *shashlik* on a grill, blaring music, and copious amounts of alcohol. These affairs will always be casual, with men and women wearing jeans or shorts, depending on the weather. You will most likely be told not to bother to bring any food, but in that case you should bring something to drink. Cold beer is a good idea. If you have any culinary aspirations, you can contribute a salad. Do not bring any meat. The men will be in charge of the grill and will have provided all that is necessary, and it may be construed as mildly insulting if you bring more meat for grilling. If you do bring a salad, make certain it is not too spicy for the Lithuanian palate. American-style potato salad is a good—and easy—way of making a contribution.

Summerhouse
The most generous invitation that can be extended is to visit someone's summerhouse. If it is a quick weekend trip, bear in mind that this is often the only time the owner will have a chance to fix things or get the place in order, and you may be put to work. You are unlikely to end up scrubbing floors, but always offer to pitch in with the chores, especially if you are female. For example, if there is a large group, the women will most certainly be cooking for some hours of the day, and offering to chop vegetables or do some of the prep work will usually  be met with a smile of approval. As pulling your weight is important in Lithuania, and foreigners are often viewed as slightly spoiled, disproving this theory will also bring you closer into a circle of friends. Men will probably have a slightly easier time of it. If the group is mixed they will be able to sit outdoors, drinking

in peace and whiling away the afternoon. If, however, your host mentions that he has been meaning to patch up a wall, you should offer to help. Men should not enter the kitchen; it will be viewed as an annoyance.

HOSPITALITY AND THANKS

Friendship in Lithuania will extinguish a certain level of formality. Invitations will often be extended no more than two weeks in advance, and usually just a few days before a party. A handwritten note or thank-you card after a lovely meal or a day at the lake will be met with puzzlement by your Lithuanian friends. Although thank-you cards are not insulting, they are not common and are still seen by many Lithuanians as a way of "putting on airs." Only in very formal situations will a thank-you note be appropriate. Lithuanians usually call the day after a party to let the host or hostess know how enjoyable the evening was and to thank them for their hospitality. For foreigners a phone call is sufficient, but should be followed up by doing your host a favor at a later date, or inviting them to your place or out to a restaurant for a meal. However, do not extend an invitation for a few weeks in case you inadvertently embark on a cycle in which both you and your newfound friend start feeling that invitations must be returned more quickly than you really wish.

Traveler's Fare

A foreign couple was out navigating the many lakes of a national park in a canoe. Growing tired from their exertions, they moored at a landing stage. The woman who owned the nearby house walked down, and as she approached them the foreigners fully expected to be told to leave her property. Instead she asked them where they were traveling to, and if they would like some fresh milk from her cow. She ran back to the house and brought them snacks to boot!

FLOWERS

Flowers have a great deal of significance. If you bring your hostess a bunch of flowers make sure it consists of an odd number of blooms. Even-numbered bouquets are solely for funerals; certain white flowers should be avoided for the same reason. Chrysanthemums and calla lilies are for funerals only, but white tulips or roses are appropriate, especially if the bouquet is for a young lady. Red carnations were used in military pageants during Soviet times and are best avoided. Yellow flowers can carry the alternative meanings of friendship or betrayal, but this is no longer a commonly held notion among the younger generation and may fall out of use very soon. With all the pitfalls there are still a few more rules to keep in mind. Women who are close friends should receive flowers on their birthdays. Foreign men should bring flowers to their sweethearts. Even small bouquets, if cheery, are considered thoughtful gifts.

In Vilnius the flower market is open around the clock. All major cities have numerous flower shops dotted about, and florists tend to be very ready to help with a decision on an appropriate bouquet. Red roses are the safest bet for a Lithuanian sweetheart. There are countless stories circulating in foreign circles in the Baltics about British or American men trying to woo Lithuanian girls by presenting an attractive bunch of yellow flowers, which their sweethearts see only as a token of friendship without any romantic ideas. One should always buy a bouquet for a birthday. Those not wanting to fall into the trap of picking the obvious should ask the florist, who will usually suggest a bunch of tulips, violets, seasonal field flowers, or freesias.

On March 8, women receive flowers as part of International Women's Day, a holiday from Soviet times that is for the most part left uncelebrated save for the purchasing of flowers. If giving female friends or coworkers flowers on this day, give only small bud roses to young women and larger roses to those over the age of fifty. Many men take this as an excuse to go out drinking after work and return home smelling of liquor with a wilted bouquet. Mother's Day is celebrated, and if you have a Lithuanian surrogate family you should give flowers to all the women with children.

GIFT GIVING

Lithuanians give gifts constantly. For foreigners it can be difficult to understand the need to bring back small tokens after every trip outside the country, but in Lithuania to return from a trip empty-handed is considered bad manners. If you stay in Lithuania for an extended period of time be aware that you will be expected to bring your Lithuanian friends gifts. Also do not be surprised if after returning to your own country your Lithuanian friends ask you to buy and mail certain items to them. Be assured that they would go to the same trouble for you.

DRINKING

Attitudes toward drink are quite different from most of Western Europe or America. Drinking copious amounts of alcohol is not considered particularly bad form. In fact it can sometimes cement relationships, as one is considered a friend after an evening of emptying bottles. The idea of the functioning alcoholic is not really understood. Alcoholics, in Lithuanian terms, are people who become derelict from drinking too much and too often, losing family members, jobs, and homes. In villages it is not uncommon for impoverished unemployed men to try to pass the time in drinking competitions; some of these have resulted in deaths. Although women do imbibe, it is more socially acceptable for a man to be drunk than a woman. Displays of public drunkenness are largely ignored. The levels of inebriation are normally not too bad as many Lithuanians have a very high tolerance. Alcohol content in beer is significantly higher than in Western Europe and the USA. In social situations a good rule of thumb is to make certain at least two people are noticeably drunker than you.

PHOTOGRAPHS

Lithuanians will often take photographs, or ask you to take one, so as to have a souvenir of an occasion. Sometimes this makes foreigners feel as if they are being mobbed by paparazzi, or filmed for a documentary. Be gracious; it is another way of including you and showing they accept you in their family or group, and it illustrates the somewhat sentimental quality that is part of the romantic streak in the Lithuanian national character.

Take a Picture

In 2004 some men were digging in the cellar of a home in Kaunas when they came upon an undetonated mine from the Second World War. They immediately realized what it was, but their first action was to go and change into suits, then return to the cellar and photograph the occasion! Only after several photographs had been taken did they call the authorities.

WHEN NOT TO HAVE AN OPINION

The standard rules apply for appropriate topics of conversation: make certain you don't insult the country or its people. For example, foreigners may find the Lithuanian culinary tradition a bit lacking, but to state what even many Lithuanians might believe to be true is bad form. The same applies to politics. Allow people to air their opinions on politics, whether it be abroad or within the country, but don't get involved in such conversations, as heated debates and uncomfortable situations can occur.

Another point of contention with Lithuanians is that they still require visas to enter certain countries, such as the USA. Voicing any sentiment that is remotely in favor of these visa requirements will see to it that you alienate all of your Lithuanian audience. Historically the country has been slighted on the world stage, having fallen under foreign rule numerous times; don't go anywhere near the topic of how Lithuania fits into the global scheme of things. If a Lithuanian starts such a conversation, they may be goading you. It is best to praise the country or change the subject.

Under no circumstances should you compare Lithuania and Poland—even to do so favorably can backfire, as it will appear that in comparing the two countries and only mentioning those ways in which Lithuania is superior you are keeping thoughts to yourself about how it is inferior! Something seemingly innocuous, such as saying that Polish women are beautiful or that a sausage you had in Warsaw was tastier than one you are eating can be construed as implied criticism, and is quite annoying. While in Lithuania, keep any fondness of Poland, and things Polish, to yourself.

Also, Lithuanians do not take kindly to any comparisons between themselves and the other Baltic nations, even if they believe that what you are saying is true. There is less tension in their relationship with Latvia, but Estonians, whose language is completely different and who are considered a variation on Finnish people, are often seen as the winners in the Baltic race toward the future. Estonians have been more systematic in making their country better known within Europe. Some Lithuanians have a slight inferiority complex in relation to Estonia. Do not broach this sensitive subject.

RACISM
Nonwhite visitors will have a difficult time traveling in Lithuania. Overt racism will not be evident in large cities for the most part, but being stared at and knowing that others are talking about you will be common experiences. In Vilnius there are many Chinese immigrants, hence the seemingly inexplicably high number of Chinese restaurants throughout the city. However, most Lithuanians cannot distinguish between

many different Asian nationalities and will refer to them all as Chinese. The term "African-American" is only used in printed media. The most politically correct term is *juodaodis*, which literally means "black skin"; however many Lithuanians use the word *negras* more frequently; neither term holds any bad connotations in the language. Nonwhite foreigners will not usually be targets of violence, but safe practices, such as not walking alone in the evenings or in desolate areas, should be adhered to. In fact, many nonwhite foreigners will be approached with curiosity. Comments or remarks that appear mildly racist should be judged by the fact that most Lithuanians have had little contact with nonwhite people. They are not usually intent on offending someone, but may simply be speaking out of ignorance.

chapter five

DAILY LIFE

THE FAMILY

Lithuanians marry young by Western European and American standards, and have often begun families by their mid-twenties. As this is also the time when many embark upon careers, having two working parents is the norm in most families. Lithuanian mothers often have the burden of bringing up the children, keeping the house, and holding down a full-time job. Luckily many have extended families or aging parents who help to take care of the children during working hours. For this reason intergenerational interaction is significantly higher than in Western Europe or the USA—why pay for day care when grandma can look after the children?

Families tend to be close-knit. Long-term health care options for the aged, other than adult children as caregivers, were virtually unheard of a decade ago, but are more widely available today. Keeping all adult family members employed is important for survival, so some families now hire outside help in the form of nurses to care for aged parents, or minders for the children.

CHILDREN

Children in Lithuania aren't coddled and are treated as small adults, so it is really only infants who hear "baby talk." However, children are well loved, and almost all Lithuanians will break into a smile when coming across children playing together. Lithuanian children are held to slightly higher standards of behavior than their American counterparts. For example, in a children's playground in the USA one might hear a mother explain that her little boy is dressed as Superman because "he won't take off the costume," but this would never occur in Lithuania. Lithuanians also tend not to schedule their children's lives in the same way that many American or British people do, such as having a set time for supper each evening. Children are occasionally brought along to late-night dinners in city establishments. They do not usually run around or misbehave, but play quietly in a corner. It has been known for children to fall asleep under the table as their parents sit and chat.

Generally speaking, Lithuanian parents tend to fret less about their children getting hurt while playing or making sure that they are in sight at all times. They are given a degree of freedom that speaks to the safety of the country. Entering courtyards in Vilnius one will often come across children playing out of doors. An adult may be inside a nearby apartment and looking out of the window occasionally to make certain they are safe, but would not sit outside on a bench to watch them every second.

Loosening the Rein

Two friends, one an American woman, the other a Lithuanian, were having lunch in Vilnius together with the Lithuanian woman's niece. The child was curious and was wandering around the restaurant surveying what was going on. At one point she was no longer visible and the American, alarmed, decided to go and look for her. Her friend laughed and said, "Do you think someone will steal this additional mouth to feed?" showing the confidence most Lithuanians have in the safety of their country for children, and also their willingness to allow them some autonomy.

TEENAGERS

Lithuanian teenagers face a very different world from that of their parents. Teenage boys can usually purchase alcohol easily; while there may be strict rules about showing documentation of one's age, there are adults who are prepared to buy alcohol for minors, to "help the lads to have some fun." The legal drinking age in bars and nightclubs is eighteen and most young men will not be allowed to enter establishments until that age, but it is common to see groups of youths drinking beer on the streets. Drugs, which were virtually impossible to get in Soviet times, have found their way into the country, although drug abuse is not yet rampant. The flood of illegal substances into the country, coupled with the blind eye turned to their infiltration into society, could spell trouble for young Lithuanians whose parents are unaware of the issues and potential signs of drug abuse. Furthermore, the same attitude of "this will not happen in our country" can be viewed in how the AIDS virus is still seen as something affecting only the homosexual population outside the country's borders. Safe sex practices are taught in schools, but among older Lithuanians condoms are still seen as a sort of novelty item.

SENIOR CITIZENS

Female retirees are the backbone of the Lithuanian state in many ways. In most populations women tend to live longer than men, but this is especially evident in Lithuania, where elderly women are seen out and about on public transportation and running errands. In fact, as many live with their married children they are often responsible for the family grocery shopping. On public transportation seats are often given up to elders. And if you are young, an older woman will generally have no qualms about telling you to vacate your seat so that she can sit down. In fact, compared to other parts of the world, older women are less marginalized across the board. For example, although measly government pensions often oblige these women to live on a dangerously low income, Lithuanians will not argue with an elder.

It is the senior population who attend religious services regularly. On Sundays many of them can be seen after Mass walking along Cathedral Square. However, churches aren't the only places for the seniors to congregate. Trying to get them socializing has been a pet project of the Vilnius mayor, Artūras Zuokas, for some time. (Some people, who are skeptical of his good intentions, claim it is easier than increasing pensions.) Although many retirees can be seen enjoying the day on park benches or strolling through any available green area, there is less chance for them to socialize in winter. In response to this the mayor, in conjunction with the Old Town restaurant association, has implemented a program whereby on certain Sundays in fall and winter retirees can have a free glass of tea or coffee at designated city establishments. The venues are listed in the newspapers along with times—normally late afternoon, when there is a dip in the number of paying patrons.

LITHUANIAN HOMES

Most Lithuanians are apartment dwellers who own rather than rent. Often the outsides of buildings look shabby in comparison to their interiors—in Vilnius some courtyards seem ready to crumble, but the apartment interiors are handsomely decorated, with modern fittings. The reason for this is that getting a group of people to agree on how to fix a communal area can be quite difficult. Starting in the late 1990s millions of dollars were spent on revitalizing the Old Town in Vilnius; streets were repaved, lamps put up, and buildings painted in soft pastel colors.

In Vilnius and in cities across Lithuania older one-story buildings are being taken down and high-rise apartment complexes are becoming the norm. Apartment complexes built during Soviet times are always an eyesore, but the newer ones tend to be more aesthetically  pleasing. However, even in new surroundings old habits die hard: Lithuanian neighbors can at times seem quite nosy. Open curtains are an invitation to look into another's apartment to see how they are living, what they have purchased, and who is coming and going.

Making a home comfortable is of the utmost priority. Large amounts of a person's income will be spent on remodeling and refurbishing their apartment to a high level of comfort. As loans are readily available for property owners, many Lithuanians take out equity loans on their apartments in order to buy appliances. Older buildings often need extensive remodeling to make sure they are habitable. Following Independence in 1991, communal bathrooms in an apartment building were not unheard of, even in the large cities. Many city dwellers invested in extending the plumbing into their apartments to give them their own bathrooms. Wealthy Lithuanians will often import goods from around the globe to give a diverse ethnic feel to their apartments, trying for something different from their neighbors.

RENTING AN APARTMENT

If you are a foreigner and do not speak Lithuanian, rent through an agency or a close friend. Finding an apartment isn't difficult, but paying one's utility bills can be. There is a special ledger in which the tenant has to note the amount of electricity used. The tenant must take this ledger to the post office and pay, although a Web-based service has also been launched. The figures are checked periodically so as to insure honesty. Paperwork, hassle, and bureaucracy can be avoided by having your landlord take care of these matters. However, a landlord coming around to check the meters will often mean a sit-down and chat that can last for some time. Tenant rights aren't strictly adhered to, so having a landlord "drop in" without calling or making an appointment isn't uncommon. Setting up a landline telephone and other services can be Kafka-esque. It is best to negotiate in the beginning with your landlord or the agency to attend to such things.

Many newer apartments aren't dependent on the centrally controlled heating systems that were the norm in Soviet times; however, some still are. The old system operates heating for the entire city. The grid is turned on after a certain temperature is reached for a number of days. This can result in buildings not being heated even if it is quite cold outside. Central heating was a good way to insure that citizens knew who was in charge in Soviet times—and living in a freezing apartment for a few days can give foreigners a glimpse into one of the colder realities of life in a Soviet country. Once the heating is turned on most apartments are overheated; however, few locals will open the windows to cool their homes down. It is always best to dress in layers in winter as outside can be freezing and interiors boiling.

Snow removal is not very regular, and entire streets remain covered in slick ice or snow. As heated pipes underneath the ground cause patches to thaw, you will often see people going a bit out of their way so as to have a less slippery walk. Many Old Town buildings in Vilnius have ice forming that can drop off and injure pedestrians. Fatalities have occurred. Exceptionally dangerous sidewalks are normally marked.

In summer, when the weather is warm enough, the hot water is often turned off for periods to repair the city's pipes. Usually a paper will be tacked on the front door of an apartment building stating (in Lithuanian) when the shutoff will occur. During this time those affected have to heat water on the stove for washing and bathing.

EVERYDAY SHOPPING

Gone are the days of the early 1990s when meat was purchased in one shop, vegetables in another, and sundries in yet another. Giant supermarkets are *de rigueur* and stock a range of products. Customer service is complemented by having restaurants, dry cleaners, locksmiths, and other facilities all in one place. In large cities these emporia are usually packed with shoppers, but in smaller towns smaller shops are still the norm. The first major retailer of foreign and local goods was the Iki supermarket chain, started soon after independence by three Belgian brother entrepreneurs. Later Maxima took over the market. In Maxima stores mobile phone batteries can be charged up and children dropped into play areas for a nominal fee. Large shopping malls are constantly being built, and a walk through one of these complexes offers a variety of shopping opportunities for clothing, groceries, and other of life's necessities. However, some small shops still exist that only sell locally produced items, and in these one has to wait in different lines for different types of products. Meats, cheeses, and the like are ordered in grams.

WORK

Lithuanians generally are hardworking—unless they are in mid- or low-level government jobs, in which case resting on laurels, earned or not, is quite common. According to a Lithuanian Statistics Department study of 2005, 59.4 percent of Lithuanian women and 66 percent of men are employed. Average gross monthly incomes range between 1,230 and 1,654 litas. Women generally earn less, sometimes for jobs where men receive higher pay for the same work. Health care is provided by the state, and a percentage is deducted from wages to pay for this. Foreigners find that even though they have paid for health care, physicians will often assume they should pay more for services rendered. The best medical care is usually received through private clinics.

A normal working day for a middle- or lower-class Lithuanian usually begins at six or seven in the morning, with a person arriving at work usually at about eight or nine. A full hour is usually taken for lunch around noon. Children will normally be let out of school anytime between one and three o'clock. The workday normally ends at around five or six, but most Lithuanians will work overtime when it is necessary, say for a large project to be completed by its deadline.

The few hours following the workday can be spent doing anything from going to a gym to picking up groceries or running errands. Young children, such as those in kindergarten, are usually picked up after six o'clock when the workday is done. Dinner is eaten some time after seven, and most Lithuanians will be settling into bed by eleven. And as elsewhere in the world, the very wealthy can afford to work less and have more leisure time.

Young Lithuanians can appear to be obsessed with working on their careers and themselves. This quest for personal betterment doesn't involve soul-searching, but translates into a well-used gym membership. The younger generation has a particularly hungry stare when eyeing the future; there is a great sense of possibility that a person can make themselves into a success story. The idea of success, though, is often very materialistic—the purchase of a fancy home, car, or wardrobe, and looking fabulous while doing it. However even with its consumerist slant, this attitude cannot be separated from its origins, which is the hope for a better future filled with prosperity.

EDUCATION
The adult literacy rates in Lithuania have remained at about a few tenths of a point below 100 percent for the last five years. Education up through the end of high school is free to all, and a minimum of ten years of schooling is required. As higher education costs aren't exorbitant, many go on to complete a university degree. Continuing education is quite popular as many companies will subsidize tuition costs.

RURAL LITHUANIA

Most foreigners only spend time in Lithuania's larger cities or on the coastal regions. And most assume that the quality of life is quite high. Although this is true for many city dwellers, life in the countryside can be quite difficult, as there are few jobs or opportunities for advancement in rural areas. That said, however, the Lithuanian countryside has some spectacular features. Locals tend to be welcoming and interested in foreign visitors who want to explore (but see overleaf on page 103, and exercise caution). Don't be surprised if you are invited in for a chat and a snack when traveling through the country. Life can be monotonous in these parts, and so anything new can create a level of interest, even if a common language is not found. Be aware that rudimentary Lithuanian language skills may not be sufficient in some parts of the country, as rural dialects can sometimes be incomprehensible, even to Lithuanians from the large cities.

Small villages can have local personalities. In fact, some of Lithuania's real charm is in its wackiness. In the Ignalina region every summer a man who calls himself Tarzanas sports a loin cloth, lives in the forest, and swings about trees and jumps into lakes; tourists pay to watch his antics. He had married his "Jane," but she joined him only for short periods for a few summers before leaving him for good.

Another woman who lives in a small village claimed that all her health troubles had been eradicated by eating sand from a local spot. The story caused many Lithuanians to groan when it was picked up by the Associated Press, but some still stop by to sample the dirt.

For all its hospitality and wackiness, the Lithuanian countryside is still quite isolated from the world. In fact some villages can be quite dangerous. Directly after Independence, the fledgling state was being haphazardly run; many changes were being implemented and no one was quite sure how to manage these or what impact they would have on people's lives. Problems arose from the slow pace of land and property restitution. As the collective farms weren't dismantled right away, some farm workers sold off animals or property but were unsure what to do with the proceeds, or whether the original owners would return to demand their property back and kick the "tenants" off their land. Still others, who had been guaranteed employment under the Soviet system, saw the factories where they worked close down, and did not know how to go about getting new jobs. Some people became lost in the new territory of democracy and started drinking heavily.

A common occurrence was for real estate agents to seek out these mentally displaced people and offer them a home in a village somewhere in return for their usually shabby apartment in a good location in Vilnius. Many accepted the offer, stayed jobless, continued to drink, and received money from the state for the maintenance of their children. There are villages with populations where most of the adults are alcoholics. In a way it was almost as if rural ghettos were being created for those who couldn't keep up with the changing times or could be easily taken advantage of. These lost souls often view themselves as the victims of change, and feel it is their right to take whatever they can from an outsider. For this reason foreigners should not go camping in areas other than those designated as safe by the national park service. Although crime rates are not high, at least one major theft occurs each summer to those traveling in remote regions of the country.

Dubious Country Welcomes

A wealthy foreigner obsessed with cleaning up national parks came to Lithuania and began to clear up litter in a park near a small village. The villagers thought he was crazy to leave a good life with money in order to pick up trash in a foreign land. The situation continued for several weeks, and the villagers would spot him at various points in the park. Soon they became angry with him, as he seemed to be choosing the impoverished lifestyle that they felt they had no choice but to live. The man eventually was attacked by a handful of locals and robbed of all his possessions.

TIME OUT

To truly understand Lithuanians you have to see
them at their most relaxed and sociable—when
on vacation, or enjoying weekends or evenings
out after work. Leisure time is usually spent with
friends or family, with a nice mixture of lazing
about and some activity. In cities, people spend a
great deal of time strolling. They walk through
parks in summer and snowed-in streets in winter;
they spend hours wandering about on weekends
and looking at new shops or seeing if any new
establishments have popped up. In summer,
sunny weekends signal a return to nature and see
many city dwellers barbecuing outdoors,
preferably by the shores of one of the country's
many lakes. Normally Lithuanian workers have
four to six weeks' vacation, and many take the
time not only to travel abroad but also to enjoy
their own country by visiting the coast.

RESTAURANTS

In large towns and cities arrays of restaurants line
the streets, offering everything from traditional
Lithuanian dishes to ethnic cuisine from all over

Europe and Asia. Lithuanian food isn't spicy and doesn't require hours of preparation, but it has a simple warmth that most people associate with their own grandmother's or home-style cooking. In smart establishments the coat check personnel can be adamant about the need for you to relinquish your coat, even if the interior is quite cool. It is considered bad manners to have your coat anywhere near your table. Women should also note that if going to upscale restaurants in snow boots they should bring along high-heeled shoes to change into in the cloakroom.

Restaurants in major cities usually have English-language menus, or at the very least members of staff who can speak English.

Lithuanian food tends to be heavy, with a focus on combining pork, cabbage, and potatoes. However, salads in the Baltic are very fresh and, together with one of the many soups to choose from, can make a light meal that is still satisfying. Generally  vegetables will be overcooked, so it is best to get them fresh in salads. Be aware that salad (*salotos*) doesn't always mean green leafy vegetables—or even any vegetables for that matter! One popular salad is *pikantiškos salotos* (spicy salad), in which cheese, hard-boiled eggs, mayonnaise, and garlic are mixed together; the "spiciness" is the result of the garlic.

Lithuanians tend to steer clear of spices, but add flavor using fresh herbs: dill is ubiquitous and even finds its way occasionally into places it doesn't belong, such as cheese pizza. Another popular herb is the base for the very tasty sorrel soup (*rūgštynių sriuba*), which also has beef stock and vegetables. The most traditional dish is *cepelinai*, a blimp-shaped boiled potato cake with meat inside. These are usually served in an order of two and are occasionally fried after boiling, to insure a very hearty meal. There are thin pancakes (*lietiniai*) with both sweet and savory fillings. Potatoes are the staple in Lithuania and are eaten as dumplings (*kugelis*) and pancakes (*bulviniai blynai*). Distinctly Lithuanian offerings are wild boar, which may be hard to find but is tasty, and local varieties of mushrooms that grow in the forests.

For main dishes pork is usually the central player. *Skilandis,* spiced ground pork meat, is placed inside a skin, usually a stomach or bladder, and then smoked. Pork rolled in egg and bread crumbs then deep-fried is called *karbonadas*. Sausages (*dešrelės*) are not spicy and are sometimes served with stewed cabbage and potatoes. Since the Baltic Sea is for the most part fished out, river and lake fish are also common. Carp (*karpis*), the traditional dish at Christmas dinner, is offered year-round as is pike (*lydeka*), herring (*silkė*), and eel (*ungurys*). Bread is served with almost every meal, and black bread is usually set on the table soon after ordering one's meal.

LET US EAT CAKE

Ladies will often be seen in cafés in small groups
chatting over coffee, tea, and most likely a dessert
of some kind. This is an important part of
cementing female relationships. If you are invited
to such a tête-a-tête, here are a few of the sweets
you will probably see on the menu or in the
display cases: buns (*pyragéliai*), cakes (*pyragas*),
doughnuts (*spurgos*). Some specific ones to try
are poppy seed cake (*pyragas su aguonomis*),
honey cake (*meduolis*), and cranberry pudding
(*spanguolių kisielius*), which has a taste both
sweet and tangy.

PLACES TO GO

Restaurants (*restoranas*) serve full meals and
occasionally offer some lighter options. For
sandwiches, salads, or something to satisfy your
sweet tooth it is best to stop by a café (*kavinė*),
bakery (*kepykla*), or milk bar (*pieno baras*). Milk
bars, which are dwindling in number, usually
have a counter where one can order a hot
beverage and a pastry. Bars (*baras*) will almost
always serve snack food too.

SUMMERTIME

Summertime is serious in the Baltic. In a region
where it can start snowing in November and
continue to be cold until April or even May,
people really appreciate it when the weather

warms up. Any establishment that can provides outdoor seating at the first sign of favorable weather. The beginning of summer is unofficially recognized by the appearance of outdoor seating and the addition to the menu of a cold beet soup (*šaltibarščiai*), which is served with a side dish of hot boiled potatoes. Because sunny days are rare, when they occur lunch breaks are often extended and people may leave work early for a quick beer in the afternoon.

DRINK
Beer

A little-known secret outside the country is just how delicious Lithuanian beer (*alus*) is—it is light and usually quite crisp, but still with a complex flavoring to it. The main brands are Horn, Kalnapilis, Švyturys, Utenos, and Tauras. Beer drinking can almost seem like a hobby (or sometimes an Olympic sport) in these climes, and most bars have a small menu of beer snacks. One of the most popular is fried sticks of black bread (*kepta duona*), which are flavored with pieces of raw garlic and occasionally topped with cheese.

Everything from peanuts (*žemės riešutai*) to smoked pig's ears (*rūkytos kiaulių ausys*) to jerky meats (*basturma*) is used to accompany the local brews.

Other Beverages

Lithuanians tend to drink beer since it is produced
in the country and is usually cheaper than bottled
water in bars and restaurants. However a few
local liquors are worth trying for those with a
sense of adventure. *Gira*, a light fermented drink
made from bread or caraway seeds, has low
alcohol content. As it is similar to the Russian
kvass the names are somewhat interchangeable.
Starka is a fruit-based liquor that is often used to
liven up one's afternoon tea. Two cranberry-based
liquors, *Palanga* and *Bobelinė*, have a medicinal
taste to them. *Trejos Devynerios* is a type of mead
that is nearly impossible to procure outside the
country. The name, which means three times
nine, is no misnomer as twenty-seven grasses,
blossoms, leaves, and roots make up the recipe.
Balzamas and *suktinis* are two other mead
alcohols, with the latter being slightly more
tolerable as it is lighter both in color and flavor.
Although wines and a champagne, Alita, are
produced in the country, none is noteworthy.

ORDERING

May I have a menu?	*Galima meniu?*
Can I have this without ... ?	*Ar galima be ... ?*
I am a vegetarian	*Aš esu vegetaras*
The bill, please	*Prašau sąskaitą (or Galima sąskaitą?)*
I would like ...	*Aš noriu ...*

NIGHTLIFE

In winter the streets of large cities can seem deserted, but ducking into one of the bars or nightclubs will prove that people are in fact out and about. Vilnius, Kaunas, and Klaipėda all have everything from small bars to large complexes with discos, casinos, and sometimes even saunas. In all three cities the centrally located bars will be fairly full from the end of the workday until ten in the evening. Nightclubs don't really pick up until after 11:00 p.m. Entrance fees are usually a nominal amount, but new clubs targeting the stylish, cool, and rich are starting to spring up. In summer most large cities have a variety of outdoor beer gardens. Smaller towns will have few options, apart from the seaside resorts in summer, where revelers can often be seen stumbling from establishment doors as the sun begins to rise.

SAFETY

Foreigners can be the targets of pickpockets, especially in bars and nightclubs where crowds and alcohol consumption can make it difficult to keep one's belongings in sight at all times. Practice vigilance. Although the country is generally safe, walking alone late at night, especially in desolate areas, is not a good idea.

SHOPPING

There are three particular kinds of souvenir worth buying while in Lithuania: amber, linen, and wood carvings. Although major cities will always have shops selling these along with other items, some of the most exciting shopping takes place on city streets at outdoor markets. Would-be purchasers should be prepared to haggle a bit. Also markets are a place where pickpockets can lurk, so it is advisable to be extra vigilant with your belongings.

Amber

Baltic amber (*gintaras*) is believed to have begun forming from 30 to 40 million years ago. The stone is in fact fossilized tree resin, and can sometimes be found with inclusions, or more precisely bugs or twigs that the resin picked up as it dripped down the tree bark. There are four types of amber found in Lithuania: white, yellow, orange/red, and green. King's, or white, amber is actually an off-white color and has some yellow swirling through it. All other varieties are the color of their names, with green amber being the rarest and therefore usually having a higher price. Most of the amber jewelry sold in Lithuania's town squares and in shops is the reddish-orange variety—and is often found in Art Nouveau settings or left as large unpolished pieces. Most amber jewelry is made into necklaces or, less commonly, earrings or rings. Amber pieces are also glued on to small paintings or stemware and sold by street vendors. When purchasing amber be aware that it is deceptively lightweight and may appear fake; rest assured, manufacturing amberlike plastics is more of a hassle than just collecting it naturally.

Most of the amber in the Baltic is found in Lithuania, particularly on the coast. Nida has a number of shops that double as museums where one can learn more about "Baltic gold." However, most medium-sized towns will have at least one shop selling amber and large cities will have several, along with street vendors.

Forever Amber

An old folktale explains how amber came to be in Lithuania. Jūratė, a beautiful mermaid, fell in love with Kastytis, a fisherman, and whisked him away to her amber castle under the Baltic Sea. As happens in such tales, their love was forbidden and the god Perkūnas sent a storm that demolished the castle in order to convey his displeasure. The pieces of the castle washed up on the shores of the Baltic—and the pieces that were in teardrop shapes are said to be the tears shed by Jūratė at the loss of her true love.

Linen

Linen (*linas*) is often used for clothing or tableware, but in Lithuania the fabric appears in bedding, dolls, and almost any type of cloth product one can imagine. Linen makes for cool clothing in summer, so even the locals can be seen wearing the fabric. This is in opposition to amber, which is rarely worn by Lithuanian women.

Some finely detailed work along the edges of linen goods can drive up the price, but one-of-a-kind items can be found quite easily in large cities. Bed linen does not appear to conform to any standard European or US size, so it is best to measure your bed before arriving in the country. The fabric, which tends to rumple with wear, can be found in the ethnic shops catering to tourists in large cities. Discounted places to buy linen do not really exist. Even if you think the pricing a bit high, be aware that the locals are not getting much of a deal on these products—the markup over the cost of production isn't that high in most cases.

Wood Carvings

The forests of Lithuania are the source of one of the country's leading tourist souvenir trades. Wood carvings are sold along roadsides, markets, and inside a handful of workshops that double as storefronts. Many of the wooden items sold at outdoor markets tend to be kitchen utensils or decorations. Devil masks are also quite popular and can be anything from absurd to mildly scary to look at. Small wooden toys for children are also easily found. Along the coast, specifically in Nida, one can purchase brightly colored wooden weather vanes made by local craftsmen.

Sashes

Ethnic costumes can also be found in tourist areas and are usually a mix of linen and cotton. A popular, affordable item that is very Lithuanian is a sash called a *juosta*, which can be as small as a bookmark and as large as a table runner. These thin sashes originally were given as a reminder of special occasions and occasionally had writing stitched into them.

CULTURE

Vilnius for the most part is the cultural seat of Lithuania, although the residents of Kaunas consider themselves the intelligentsia and theirs the more Lithuanian of the two cities. Both offer a range of theater performances, which will always be in the Lithuanian language—so foreigners are best off attending concerts. Tickets are relatively inexpensive by US and Western European standards, but performances are not always of a very high caliber. Symphony performances will often have the well-heeled and older Lithuanian set in attendance.

In summer most major cities host a variety of music festivals, with concerts often held in churches. Stop by the local tourist office to find out what is on.

SPORTS

Lithuanians have two great loves: nature and basketball. And the love of basketball can often verge on the fanatical. Sports, both watched and participated in, are important part of the culture. Although many Lithuanians smoke cigarettes and ingest high amounts of alcohol and fatty foods, most are relatively healthy. The reasons for this could be that food portions are not huge, Lithuanians walk more than Americans, and they take part in more activities that qualify as exercise.

In winter, ice sports are popular. Lithuanians will find any hill large enough to sled down, and enjoy cross-country skiing over the terrain, which is never too mountainous. Skating, at indoor ice rinks or outside, often gets the entire family out showing off their fancy footwork for a few hours. In summer the lakes attract swimmers, canoers, and bikers, who all enjoy the pristine beauty of the national parks throughout the country.

Basketball
Basketball is the national pastime. Lithuanians are proud of their feats in the sport and Šarūnas Marčiulionis is treated almost as a national hero. He and Arvydas Sabonis helped the USSR secure the gold medal for basketball at the 1988 Olympics. He then went on to play in the American NBA for the Portland Trailblazers. Later he helped lead the Lithuanian basketball team in the 1992 Summer Olympics; some credit him with resurrecting the team entirely. One sponsor of

the team was none other than the San Francisco-based group the Grateful Dead, who fitted out the Lithuanians in tie-dyed warm-up suits in the national colors. The Lithuanian Olympic basketball team won bronze medals in 1992, 1996, and 2000. Their winning of the European championships guaranteed their place at the 2004 Olympic games, where they came in fourth place. Lithuania also won the EuroLeague championships in 1999. The best-known national team is the Žalgiris team, but the Vilnius Lietuvos Rytas have begun to make a name outside the country. The Lietuvos Rytas (also the name of a Lithuanian daily) are based in Vilnius, whereas Žalgiris is based in Kaunas. Games tend to be raucous and quite fun.

Sports for Visitors
In the last decade Lithuanian entrepreneurs have realized that there is a market for rich locals and foreign visitors to enjoy adventure sports. The vast amount of unspoiled countryside means that today anything can be done, for a price—from shooting wild boar to firing off an AK-47 Kalashnikov, to skydiving, to flying in a trick airplane, or driving an off-road vehicle. Bungee jumping off Vilnius's TV tower is another highlight of an adventure trip. Paintball and go-karting are also popular.

More low-key winter activities include ice fishing, cross-country skiing, indoor ice skating, sledding, and renting snowmobiles. Renting

canoes and meandering through the country's many lakes or rivers is another way both locals and visitors get to see the countryside in summer. Golfing and racket sports are gaining popularity in the large cities, and there are growing numbers of venues in which to enjoy them. There are three golf courses in the country, but more are likely to spring up as the game seems to be gaining in popularity.

chapter seven

TRAVELING

Traveling in Lithuania is relatively hassle-free as the country is quite small and the road system is well developed and maintained. In general train travel is best for destinations outside the country; within Lithuania buses are the fastest and cheapest form of transport. If your language skills are shaky, write down your travel dates and destination on a piece of paper and show it at the ticket office when purchasing tickets so as to lessen the likelihood of an incorrect ticket being issued. Dates are written with the day first, followed by the month, followed by the year.

ARRIVAL

Most visitors arriving by air usually fly in to Vilnius International Airport. However Amber Air runs a few flights from Kaunas, usually via Palanga, to and from destinations in Germany and Scandinavia. There are no direct flights from the USA or Australia. Vilnius airport's arrival hall is small, but has a 24-hour baggage-storage area, a 24-hour currency exchange office, and public telephones. Outside there are plenty of cabs.

Taxis are metered, but prices fluctuate and are slightly higher on national holidays and in the evenings. Although tips are not necessary, it is customary to round up the figure to the nearest lita or two. Tourists will usually be charged an inflated rate— recent changes mean that one company has a monopoly on airline pickups as most of its drivers speak a nominal amount of English. The price difference for most Westerners will be negligible, but if you are intent on getting the lowest price your best bet is to arrange for a pickup by your hotel, or to call for a cab.

IMMIGRATION AND CUSTOMS

Immigration and customs was a relatively fast process even before EU accession, and remains so. There are no restrictions on goods brought in from EU countries, although anything more than 10,000 litas in cash must be declared. If you are arriving from a nonmember state, make sure your gifts for your Lithuanian friends do not exceed the limit of one bottle of hard liquor or two liters of beer or wine, 200 cigarettes, or 50 g of perfume.

EU residents can stay in Lithuania for as long as they wish, but if they plan on working or living in the country on a permanent basis they must obtain a resident's permit before entering the country. Travelers from Australia, New Zealand, Scandinavia, Switzerland, and the USA do not require entrance visas; however, for each country there is a different limit on the length of time their citizens can stay, ranging from thirty to ninety days.

GETTING AROUND
By Rail
Long distances are usually best covered by trains. Overnight trains have different classes of tickets. Shared compartments will guarantee you a seat only, whereas four-person compartments have beds. Women traveling alone should be aware that they could be placed in a compartment with three men. Each carriage has its own manager and usually speaking with them can get your accommodation altered. Most train staff speak Lithuanian, Polish, and Russian, and sometimes they have a smattering of English and German.

Traveling by train in general will result in some small talk being started by others in your compartment. If a mutually understandable language is found do not be surprised by lengthy conversations. Those opposed to chatting are advised to bury their nose in a book. In the morning tea or coffee will usually be served.

By Bus
Bus travel is by far the fastest option within the republic. Regular buses connect all the major cities and coastal resorts. However buses do vary in quality and comfort. Pan-Baltic buses or those

connecting large cities tend to be the nicest and newest, whereas those heading for Kaliningrad or Poland tend to be older vehicles barreling down the highways. The assigned seating is not always adhered to. If another passenger has taken your seat simply show your ticket to the driver and look lost; they will jettison the person from your seat. Pit stops will be fairly frequent, but one must pay to use the restrooms, though ostensibly the charge is for toilet paper, so keep small change in your pocket.

By Plane
Most travel within the country is done by car or bus; however, in summer there are cheap flights between Palanga and both Vilnius and Kaunas. Many take advantage of the low fares to enjoy time on the coast without the aggravation of having to pilot themselves there.

By Car
Renting a car allows you to explore more of the country and on your own personal timetable. Main roads, such as the A2, connecting Vilnius and Riga, or the A1, connecting Vilnius and Klaipėda, are a joy to drive along. In rural areas it is not uncommon to have horse-drawn carriages or tractors slowing down the traffic. Potholes and dirt roads are also to be found in such areas.

Drivers are more aggressive than in the USA or Western Europe. However, even if the Lithuanian driving style seems erratic and somewhat dangerous there are rules one should adhere to.

Use the left lane only to pass slower-moving traffic. Headlights should be on at all times. If you are involved in an accident, no matter how minor, do not move your vehicle until the police arrive. Do not drink and drive; drivers with a level of alcohol in the bloodstream of 0.04 percent or more are subject to arrest. Most signage will be familiar to visitors from Europe.

Speed limits as a general rule are as follows: 31 to 37 mph (50 to 60 kmph) in towns and cities, 55 mph (90 kmph) on country roads, and 62 mph (100 kmph) on the Vilnius–Kaunas freeway. Be aware that a town's speed limit applies up until the point where a sign with the town's name is crossed out in red. Speed traps are set up in seemingly rural areas that are within the town's perimeter as drivers tend to speed up in a less populated area. When traveling on a two-lane road, if a person flashes their lights at you it is a warning that police are making stops up ahead and you should slow your vehicle down to the speed limit. (It will be assumed that you are speeding, as everyone does.) If you are flagged down by a police officer, pay the fine on the spot as otherwise you will have to go to a police station later in order to clear the ticket.

Parking in Vilnius Old Town, central Kaunas, and in Palanga during the summer holidays can verge on the nightmarish. When traveling to these destinations it is best to leave your vehicle at a hotel or out-of-the-way spot, and use public transportation, or taxis, or walk.

LOCAL TRANSPORTATION
Public Transportation
In the large cities public transportation is well developed. A variety of buses, such as minibuses and trolleys, jam the streets. In Vilnius bus tickets can be purchased at kiosks and are valid for a single journey, no matter the distance. The eldest in the public transport family is the trolleybus (powered by an overhead wire); many of these are being phased out. Buses, which are state-owned, are slightly more nimble than trolleybuses. The speediest way around town is on private minibuses that run routes similar to the trolley and bus lines; their destinations are written on a placard on the front of the bus. In order to board a minibus one must flag it down, hand money to the driver or other passengers who will pass it to the driver, and then let the driver know when you want to get off. In Kaunas a ride on one of the city's funiculars provides a lovely way to revisit the past and avoid hiking up the city's steep hills.

Taxis
If you are foreign and do not speak Lithuanian you should come to terms with the fact that when you flag down taxis you will be charged more than a Lithuanian citizen. The increase won't be more than a few litas. It is always better to call for a cab. Many cab operators will speak some English; you can also ask bar, hotel, or restaurant staff to call one for you. When you order a taxi

you will be given the number of the car. If your destination is a particular address—rather than a hotel or venue—then it is best to write it down on a piece of paper to hand to the driver. Taxi rates on holidays and at night are slightly higher. Tipping is not required, but one should round up the fare to the nearest litas or two.

DESTINATIONS

Lithuania is not home to any of the wonders of the world. That being said, it has a distinctive charm of its own, particularly evident in its many architectural styles and its museums dedicated to interesting, if not sometimes downright odd, themes. Its two greatest delights are the winding streets of Vilnius's Old Town and its visually arresting natural beauty.

Vilnius

Vilnius's Old Town, a UNESCO World Heritage Site, is hands down the crown jewel of the country's tourism industry. Its small size makes exploring on foot a pleasant way to spend a day, as slim streets wind, cross, and unravel through the 887-acre (359-hectare) area. The Old Town is adjacent to the city center and everything is within walking distance; Cathedral Square connects the two areas and is usually a hive of activity. The cathedral is quite large, with its focal point being the chapel of St. Casimir. Numerous miracles are attributed to him and worshipers leave silver ornaments depicting ailing body parts as votive offerings.

Looking down on to Cathedral Square is Gediminas Hill, home to the Upper and Lower Castles that provide a lovely vantage point from which to view the city. An elevator makes the upward journey that much simpler. The bell tower is usually lit up at night and many people stroll along the perimeter of the square in the evenings to enjoy the view. The rest of Old Town is also delightful. With the weighty buildings of Vilnius University acting as an anchor, poking around its courtyards and buildings

allows for some interesting architectural finds.

Gedimino prospektas is the main artery of the city center, starting from the cathedral and ending at the Neris River. The street is lined with shops, restaurants, and the city's former KGB headquarters, where ex-inmates take you through the underground prison.

Churches

One of the main points of reference in Vilnius is the sixteenth-century Gates of Dawn, (Aušros Vartai). The Gates of Dawn are a former city wall containing a chapel that houses a large icon of the Virgin, believed to have miracle-working powers. Pilgrims can often be seen prostrating themselves on the stone steps leading up to the chapel.

The city is filled with churches; most are Roman Catholic and are open during the day. A few of note include the Orthodox Church of the Holy Spirit (Stačiatikių Šventosios Dvasios Cerkvė), which houses the bodies of three martyrs (Saints Anthony, Eustachius, and Ivan).

As it is believed they have healing powers, the bodies are displayed naked in glass cases on June 26 to be venerated by the faithful. The adjacent Church of St. Teresa (Šv. Teresės Bažnyčia), one of the oldest churches in the city, is down the street from the Gates of Dawn. The façade is striking for its stone scrolls, which appear to hang like fabric. The interior of the Church of Sts. Peter and Paul (Švs. Petro ir Povilo Bažnyčia) is decorated with thousands of white stucco fixtures. An enormous boat-shaped chandelier hangs down into the middle of the church.

The Dominican Church of the Holy Spirit (Šventosios Dvasios Bažnyčia) serves the Polish community; inside the main fresco is breathtaking with its rings of clouds sailing up through the heavens. St. Anne's Church, which according to legend Napoleon wished to take back to France in the palm of his hand, is a sixteenth-century red-brick building constructed from thirty-three different kinds of bricks.

Užupis

The "Montmartre of Vilnius" houses many artists and more than a handful of oddities and curiosities. Some residents of this neighborhood have gone so far as to declare themselves a breakaway republic, whose independence day is celebrated on April 1. On this day a tongue-in-cheek display commences with border patrols set up around the neighborhood where "policeman" check documents and stamp passports. The republic claims to have an ambassador in Moscow and an army of twelve men. Their constitution, which can be seen on the eastern beginning of Paupio Street, is written on a mirrored surface in both English and Lithuanian. The only requirement of citizens is that they remember their names. The famous Užupis Café sees many of the citizens and "freedom fighters" enjoying cocktails or coffee on its outdoor area in summer. Adjacent to the café is the usually deserted  Alternative Arts Center (Alternatyvaus meno centras), which is the acting headquarters for the Užupis Ministry of Culture. A walk along the river path from the building can lead to the discovery of pieces of sculpture. Throughout the neighborhood there are many small workshops.

Outdoor Parks

Its many outdoor parks are what make Lithuania a charming place to visit. Most are located close enough to Vilnius to be a day trip. Trakai is less than 18 miles (28 km) from Vilnius, and many visit the early fifteenth-century Island Castle situated on Lake Galvė. It is best to visit during warm weather if you want to enjoy boat rides or wind sailing on the lake. Trakai's castle also has a museum dedicated to the history of the area. An interesting detour is to check out the local Karaite community. Originally from the Black Sea area, they have an ethnographic museum and a few traditional restaurants in the town.

Europos Parkas and the nearby Center of Europe are just two of the decidedly wacky places to spend an afternoon outside Vilnius. French National Geographic Institute members established the center of Europe here in Lithuania. The point is marked by a statue and museum that for the most part only sells documentation that you have in fact been to the center of Europe. More interesting is the Europos Parkas, where artists have created outdoor sculptures of their conceptions of the center of Europe. This gigantic park is located 10.5 miles (17 km) outside Vilnius. It has a restaurant, a post office, and a meadow with three metal and rope structures. These are intended for use by visitors and with the aid of a friend will have you spinning around in a piece of art. The structures seem safe enough if a certain velocity is maintained and the rider holds on for dear life.

Grūto Parkas, near the spa resort of Druskininkai in the south, is a collection of former Soviet public statuary from throughout the country. The park is equidistant from Vilnius and Kaunas, situated at about 74.5 miles (120 km) from both. It was designed so that one can roam for quite some time before happening upon a large statue. It can be an eerie experience. Stirring Soviet music is broadcast from guard towers. There is a small café and a museum of Soviet propaganda, along with a playground.

The outdoor ethnographic museum Rumšiškės is about 12 miles (20 km) outside Kaunas. The 435-acre (176-hectare) grounds contain examples of traditional housing and farming implements from Lithuania's four regions: Žemaitija, Dzūkija, Aukštaitija, and Suvalkija. The typical wooden and thatched-roofed houses are surrounded by grasses and trees that are indigenous to their region. Artisans can be seen in their workshops and during holiday weekends performances and festivities may be held here.

Kaunas

Kaunas is Lithuania's second-largest city. Its Old Town, though not as charming as Vilnius, is still lovely for strolling. The historic heart of the city is its Town Hall Square, Rotušės aikštė, which is surrounded by sixteenth-century German

merchant houses. The town hall is nicknamed "the White Swan" for its elegant lines. The pulse of Kaunas cannot really be taken without having strolled down Laivės aleja; the numerous shops, restaurants, cafés, and bars lining the street and flanking its offshoots insure that an entire day could be spent wandering here. The street ends at the Church of St. Michael the Archangel, a truly beautiful Byzantine-style church. The Mykolas Žilinskas Art Museum across the square has Lithuania's only Rubens. The entrance is marked by a statue of a very naked man who has scandalized some residents since 1991.

Klaipėda

The country's third largest city, the seaport of Klaipėda, has its own distinct flavor and a marked Prussian influence that can be seen in its symmetrical street plan and many *Fachwerk* (half-timbered) homes. The city is built on both sides of the mouth of the Danė River. The Old Town is rather small. One of the more interesting spots to visit is the Blacksmith's Museum, a smithy where one can watch workers forge iron. Other places to visit include the Clock Museum, which houses everything from sundials to atomic clocks, and Mažvydos sculpture park.

Šiauliai

The Hill of Crosses is located about 7.5 miles (12 km) outside Šiauliai, the fourth-largest city. As this is no misnomer, expect to see thousands of crosses covering a hillside. People started planting the crosses in around 1850, and they continue to do so. The Soviets bulldozed the site numerous times, but the crosses kept reappearing. The large Jesus statue was a gift from Pope John Paul II during his 1993 visit.

Off the Beaten Path

In the village of Gargždelė is the Orvidas Farmstead Museum, which is run by Vilius Orvydas, a rather eccentric naive artist who has a collection of artworks that run the gamut from strange to serious. A great deal of religious work is also displayed in this open-air museum, along with Soviet-era artifacts that the artists have managed to salvage. Further north in the town of Mosėdis is the Museum of Unique Rocks, which houses a collection of more than 20,000 rocks, ranging from boulders to stones, gathered from neighboring countries. The reasoning behind the museum has never been explained.

The Coast

Palanga is a seaside resort about 25 miles (40 km) north of Klaipėda. Its beaches are packed in summer, when city dwellers from all over the country descend upon it, as nearly everyone has a friend or relative with a summerhouse in the area.

Bars, nightclubs, and restaurants seem to spring up overnight. Popular activities include sunbathing, eating, drinking, and strolling. In fact, the entire town can seen sauntering along the pier or waterfront at sunset to enjoy the view. There is an old Lithuanian joke that you should never walk along the pier at sunset with a secret lover—as you are sure to be caught! A botanical garden

surrounds the Amber Museum that explains everything about the resin. At the Antanas Mončys House Museum viewers are allowed to touch every piece of sculpture as the artist instructed in his will.

Natural Beauty

Lithuania has a great deal of natural beauty to offer, and boasts four national parks. Aukštaitijos National Park, with its 200-plus interconnected lakes and acres of conifer forests, is perfect for canoe and camping trips. Inside the park the Bee-keeping Museum in Stripeikiai village allows visitors to sample honey and view hives in the shapes of pagan gods. Mushroom and berry pickers have a field day in Dzūkija National Park's pine forests. The Curonian Spit National Park (Kuršių Nerija National Park) is located on a sliver of sand flanked by the Baltic Sea on one side and the Curonian Lagoon on the other.

The Curonian Spit

The Curonian Spit is a mile-wide slice of land covered by sand dunes that rises to about 200 feet (60 m) and extends over 60 miles (97 km). Only the northern portion is in Lithuania; the rest is in the Russian enclave of Kaliningrad. The dunes are subject to shifting due to winds and in the recent past entire villages have been buried. Dutch doors on the fishing cottages point to the need to be able to get out of a house should sand block the exit. An outdoor wooden sculpture park in Juodkrantė is dedicated to wood carvings of characters from folklore. Witches' Hill, Raganų Kalnas, is surrounded by a pine forest.

This fairy-tale landscape can only be reached by barges that run between it and the mainland. Four sleepy fishing outposts are dotted along the 27-mile (45-km) road that winds its way through the park. The largest settlement, Nida, is unique and inspiring. Lithuanians often partially joke that Nida's beauty and the fragility of the landscape forces one to draw parallels with the human experience, causing a person to take stock of their life. Visitors are not allowed to walk on the dunes and must keep to paths in order to help protect the fragile ecosystem.

Nida offers the most options for travelers. A small re-created fisherman's house gives one a glance into the

lives of the intrepid people who live here. Amber is found throughout this region, and there are a museum and numerous shops in the main part of town. Those seeking sun or quiet head out to the beaches, which are often separated by gender and allow naked sunbathing. Men crossing women-only beaches should stick close to the water and not loiter—otherwise half-clothed grannies will give them a piece of their mind. Nida has discos and bars in the summer, but most visitors come to enjoy a quiet and relaxed atmosphere.

WHERE TO STAY

The hotel industry in Lithuania is probably one of the best illustrations of how large chains and mom-and-pop operations can create niche markets and still survive. Most hotels will welcome children, but pets are less likely to get a warm reception. Breakfast is usually included in pricing at mid-range options, but not always in upmarket or budget accommodation. Seasonal price fluctuations are expected along the coast, but not necessarily in larger cities. Travelers with disabilities may experience some difficulties, as hotels that promote themselves as being wheelchair friendly (and are, on the inside) often have steps up to the entrance. Many hotels now offer online booking. Big hotels tend not to be filled to capacity unless there are large groups or a convention. If you arrive with nowhere to stay, a quick stop at the local tourist information office can usually solve the problem.

Upscale Accommodation

The prices of four-star hotels in the large cities will be in line with Western European mid-range hotels. Big-name chains such as the Radisson can be found in Vilnius, Kaunas, and Klaipėda. Boutique hotels have caught on as a way of luring in travelers. Large behemoth hotels that were part of the Soviet era have been revamped, offering all amenities from restaurants to bars to nightclubs in one large complex. Many upscale hotels will have comforting touches, such as heated bathroom tiles and towel rails.

Mid-range Accommodation

Mid-range hotels tend to be safe and feature a few creature comforts, but lack personality when part of a larger chain. If a clean room located in a nice neighborhood is all you require, these are your best bet. The best way to find a mid-range hotel that has some character is to ask around.

Budget Accommodation

By far the cheapest and most charming forms of accommodation are the bed and breakfasts. Some are in private homes, others are self-contained apartments. Litinterp has offices in most areas and can help with securing either type of accommodation—and also rental cars. Large cities will always have a youth hostel too, but price structuring often means that bed and breakfast in a private home is not much more expensive.

BUSINESS BRIEFING

The Lithuanian economy has been moving
forward at a steady pace since Independence.
GDP grew by 7.5 percent in 2005, according to a
UNESCO report. In 2006 it was $30.2 billion.
Inflation is low. Many economists forecast that
EU membership will have
further positive repercussions
on the economy. The country
has had a liberal trade policy
since before EU accession,
attracting many foreign
investors, primarily from
Germany, Denmark, Estonia,
Finland, Russia, and Sweden.

The main economic sectors
are manufacturing, wholesale
and retail trade, transport and
communications, real estate, renting, and business
activities. The main exports are mineral products,
machinery, electrical equipment, textile and
textile articles, and to a lesser degree wood and
wood products. Lithuania's location has turned
the country into a transport hub, while its
educated workforce has been a valuable resource

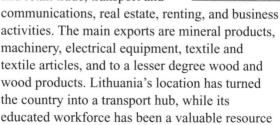

of technological know-how. The information technology sector is growing rapidly, and the republic is gaining international recognition for its advances in biotechnology and laser technology. IT services are also provided in both foreign and domestic markets.

YOUNG AND BRIGHT

Company structures and management styles vary. There are large inefficient bureaucracies, which is often the case in state-run agencies, and small companies where consensus, delegation, and cooperation are the touchstones. What is evident in business interactions with Lithuanians is their optimism about future growth, not only of their own company but of the economy as a whole.

Visitors to Lithuania will notice that although advanced years appear to be a prerequisite for holding office in government, many young Lithuanians hold primary positions in the workforce. Whereas in America people tend not to realize their potential as adults until the age of thirty or so, Lithuanians are considered adult by the age of eighteen. Many companies in large cities offer tuition incentive programs that allow employees to obtain higher degrees while remaining at work. The average Lithuanian is better educated than his or her American or British counterpart. Those with business degrees tend to have a more interdisciplinary approach to life and are well-versed in art and music.

Starting up a new business in Lithuania is relatively easy compared to neighboring countries. Many banks are willing to fund new ventures. According to a 2006 World Bank report, in Lithuania the average number of procedures involved in starting a business was seven, and the time taken to get a company officially running was twenty-six days.

BUSINESS ETIQUETTE
Punctuality
Lithuanians are not rigidly punctual, but arriving more than ten minutes late for a meeting will be taken as a mild insult unless you call to say that you are running late. Being early for meetings or appointments is considered slightly annoying.

Formality
When meeting business partners formality is key, and may continue for a long time. Lithuanians will use the most polite forms of address with one another, and if someone is your superior you should do the same until they broach the subject of using first names. Follow the lead of the people you are meeting and do not hand out business cards until they do.

Formal business dress is *de rigueur*. Showing up in casual clothing, even if smart, is not a good idea as it shows lack of respect for the people you are meeting. However, this formality does not extend to the way Lithuanians generally meet in conference rooms—sitting at round tables with the participants facing one another—where a relaxed and cooperative spirit is encouraged by the seating arrangements. Coffee or tea, and sometimes cookies, will almost always be offered. So even in the context of a rather formal occasion there are lighter touches that add a personal dimension to business interactions.

Outside the Conference Room

Colleagues or business partners may have occasion to introduce their wives or husbands at social events. When two male colleagues introduce their wives to each other both women will give a slight head nod and a softly spoken, "*Labai malonu*," or "Nice to meet you." Handshakes are generally reserved for men, but women in senior positions will shake the hands of male colleagues.

In wealthier business circles a trend has begun of discussing business over a game of golf or while hunting. Normally such an invitation will be extended only after many meetings, unless, of course, your Lithuanian counterpart really wants to impress you early on. Some casual meetings take place at local restaurants or bars, in which case they will probably involve drinking alcohol. Lunch or dinner meetings are usually reserved for tying up the loose ends of a deal.

If you invite a Lithuanian business contact out for a meal it is understood that you will be paying. Especially with older and high-level management, it is best to pick an upscale restaurant. If you are an important client for a Lithuanian business, especially a private one, anticipate that at some point you will be invited home for a meal that can last for many hours. If business ties become very close, an invitation to spend a weekend at one's summerhouse is usually extended to foreign guests.

MEETINGS
Setting up a Meeting
In general when scheduling meetings try to avoid the summer months entirely, especially as many city dwellers will be absent for four- to six-week periods. Also keep track of national holidays; if you mention to a prospective Lithuanian partner that a particular day might not work for them as it is a specific holiday you will gain their respect.

Protocol and Presentations
As hierarchy is important make certain when attending meetings that everyone is aware of everyone else's title. You should wait to be seated if meeting in a conference room as often people of similar rank will be placed directly across the table from one another by the organizer.

Most business meetings will start with small talk. It is in these initial moments that a "gut decision" will usually be made by your Lithuanian counterparts as to whether or not they feel they can do business with you and consider you a trustworthy individual. Steer clear of any stories that could be seen as a slight on the country or its people.

Make certain you have plenty of business cards; every person at the meeting should receive one along with any handouts accompanying your presentation. Your card should clearly state your position in the company. Lithuanians attach great importance to higher degrees. If you can mention your own academic credentials, or that you attended a well-known university, seamlessly and without sounding boastful, then do so.

During the meeting make sure you maintain eye contact with people in the room. The Lithuanian lack of physical touch is more than compensated for by a level of eye contact that some foreigners feel borders on staring. Lithuanians will be more quietly spoken than Americans, and their conversation may seem to meander at first. Keep a physical distance of an arm's length. If getting up to speak or present information, do not put your hands in your pockets as it is considered rude.

Detailed, step-by-step presentations will hold an audience better than those dealing with the "big picture." Most Lithuanian businesspeople will be interested in how plans are to be implemented and may want to go into details, even if it seems far too early

for such a discussion. Be prepared to delve
rather deeply into the mechanics of a plan when
presenting it.

NEGOTIATIONS

Lithuanians, especially those under the age of
thirty, are aggressive negotiators. Many
executives over the age of fifty exhibit sneaky or
mildly duplicitous behavior in negotiation—
having been schooled in the Soviet-era when
getting anything done required a degree of low
cunning. When large amounts of money are at
stake expect tough bargaining. At the same time,
flexibility will also be shown by Lithuanian
businesspeople, many of whom pride themselves
on the ability to find a happy medium. In most
negotiations they will be assertive on their
position, but willing to entertain ideas that will
strike a balance for both parties.

Generally speaking, nothing is accomplished
in one or two meetings. However thorough you
are when presenting information, no amount of
preliminary work on your part will speed up a
decision. If you feel you are being unnecessarily
delayed, you probably aren't wrong. While there
will be need for detail on your part, the
Lithuanians will generally
not give a direct response
after one meeting. The
decision to enter into
business with someone

is a considered one; it usually takes several meetings and conversations before any progress is made. It is in your best interest never to let on if your company has a deadline, because if it passes and a deal is secured after the closing date, your "deadlines" will never be taken seriously in the future. Always leave plenty of time to work out the details of any deal.

Often you will find that even though you have been told you are speaking with a person who can authorize a deal, it will later be explained that someone higher up the chain of command has to look it over. Sometimes this will be presented as your fault. For example, a Lithuanian associate might claim that a small part of a plan that was never mentioned in initial e-mails or phone calls now puts the deal partially in someone else's jurisdiction. Another common way of stalling is to blame external factors that will not be adequately explained. Many foreigners find these delaying tactics extremely annoying, but it would be wrong to regard them as sinister or mean-spirited. They are a sign of caution. Their purpose is to buy time so that the Lithuanians can be certain that they do in fact want to do business with you. They point to the Lithuanian need to deal with people whom they like or trust.

CONTRACTS
Contracts conform to the laws of the republic of Lithuania and are written in the Lithuanian

language; however, foreign businesspeople should be able to receive a translated version. As in most parts of the world contracts are binding, and are only as good as the lawyers who have drawn them up. Lithuanians respect contracts, but it is best to keep companies engaged in regard to deadlines: most will meet them punctually.

Late payments of more than a day are frowned upon, but do occasionally occur. Foreigners who find they may be late in paying or fulfilling a contract should try to give as much notice of this as possible to their Lithuanian business partner, and very definite dates for when their obligation will be fulfilled. Foreigners should contact their Lithuanian counterparts the day after a contract agreement has not been fulfilled.

CORRUPTION

Bribery, we have mentioned, is a part of daily life. But this should be seen in proportion. Lithuania's rating is 4.8 on Transparency International's corruption index, according to which any score higher than 5.0 indicates a serious corruption problem. In 2005 the Lithuanian chapter of Transparency International found that most bribes were cash given in the hopes of expediting a service. Less commonly, gifts were given to thank someone after a service had been received. Doing business in Lithuania generally will not require foreigners to bribe officials or public servants, but may have their subordinates doing so.

WORKING WITH LITHUANIANS

Western managers with Lithuanian subordinates will find that clear communication helps to overcome potential problems caused by cultural differences or social mores. Lithuanians are used to working with foreigners and may write off any behavior on your part that strikes them as rude or incorrect as just a part of your "foreignness."

Lithuanian bosses tend not to be effusive with praise, but usually congratulate employees when they have done something beyond the strict requirements of the job. Praising work won't create an air of complacency; it will often get your employees working harder to impress you.

Lithuanians like any reason to celebrate. Make certain to keep track of office workers' birthdays so that you can contribute to a small celebration by bringing a cake, sweets, or even champagne, as enjoying a late afternoon tipple in the office is still not frowned upon in most places. Male Lithuanian bosses will usually join the festivities, but not offer more than a bunch of flowers or chocolates should it be a female employee. Female bosses usually bring in something for everyone to enjoy.

When dealing with personnel issues, Lithuanians are not confrontational. They understand that sometimes a situation should not be openly stated or aired in public. There are several reasons for this. One is that it allows a person to save face; for example, a person will appear not to have been removed from a project but moved to a different one, when in reality they have been dismissed. Also, companies may keep two sets of books so as to have small reserves of petty cash that they can use for minor expenses, without needing to obtain multiple permissions. When dealing with Lithuanian employees who are unhappy with a decision, it is almost always better to state the company line, but to intimate that if the decision had been up to you completely then perhaps the situation would have be different. This will not be seen as weakness on your part, but will cement the idea that you are a benefactor whose hands are tied.

Taking the time to get to know partners and coworkers is of the utmost importance. Some Westerners feel that they have to wait ages for the formality at work to dissipate into something more comfortable. Patience is needed.

Much can be accomplished if you establish a good working relationship by having a drink and a chat with colleagues. Lithuanians are the most talkative of all the Baltic peoples, and being approachable will earn you their respect. A Lithuanian colleague's invitations should always be received graciously, even if the activity sounds tiresome or a bit too close, such as viewing photographs of their vacation or going to a communal sauna. Consider these acts rites of passage that will bring you closer to them. If you are unable to attend an event, try to make up for it by scheduling some other activity instead.

PERSONAL CONTACTS

Lithuanians have a cooperative spirit and will go out of their way to help friends or family. Personal connections are important and often determine how successful a person is. Few can survive life in Lithuania without a few hands to help them. Foreigners, once they have jumped the hurdles and established a good rapport with coworkers, are amazed by how people always have a friend or relative who can help, even with personal issues. Reciprocally, you may be called upon for favors. Some foreigners feel as if they are always being asked to do some small favor; however, one can easily discern who is a true friend by seeing if the favors are ever returned.

WOMEN IN BUSINESS

The glass ceiling that many Western women face is more of a cement wall in Lithuania. Not only are many high-level executive positions not open to women, but women are paid a portion of what a man would receive for similar work. Laws exist to stop harassment or unfair hiring practices, but they are not always adhered to and litigation for unfair business practices toward women is virtually unheard of. Even in hiring staff, employers may sometimes choose a man over a woman as young women, particularly in their twenties, are seen as likely to become pregnant and take time off.

chapter nine

COMMUNICATING

LANGUAGE

Lithuanian is spoken by about three and a half million people in the country, in certain border areas of Poland and Belarus, and by émigrés abroad, particularly in the United States. One of the two surviving Baltic languages (Latvian is the other), it is the oldest living Indo-European language, closely related to Sanskrit (ancient Indian). It was the French linguist Antoine Meillet who stated that "anyone wishing to hear how Indo-Europeans spoke should come and listen to a Lithuanian peasant." Lithuanian has changed over time, but has retained features that linguists consider archaic. Words and phrases have crept in from English, German, Polish, and Russian over time.

The four distinct cultural regions of Lithuania all have their own dialects; however the Lithuanian spoken in the streets of major cities is based on the Aukštaičių dialect, specifically the Suvalkiečių dialect. The other offshoots of the Aukštaičių dialect are Rytų Aukštaičių (commonly just called Aukštaičių) and Dzūkų.

The native speakers whom most Lithuanians have difficulty in understanding are those who speak a pronounced Žemaičių dialect. The Dzūkų dialect, though different, doesn't cause significant hardship for standard Lithuanian speakers.

Learning Lithuanian is daunting for foreigners. There are seven cases, five declensions, and the language is rendered unintelligible should the stress be placed on the incorrect vowel. There are also a few letters that may be unfamiliar. The characters *c*, *s*, and *z* can appear with a *háček* over them, which renders *č* into a "ch" sound, *š* into a "sh" sound, and *ž* into a "zh" sound. As Lithuanian is a synthetic, rather than analytic, language meaning is derived from word endings rather than their syntactic order in a sentence.

Lithuanians will be very impressed if you have a slight knowledge of their grammar and pronunciation. Even learning to say "please" and "thank you" in their language will be appreciated.

Picking a Language
Lithuanians are well aware not only that most visitors will not speak their language, but that even if they live in the country for a significant period they will not bother to learn more than a few pleasantries. The foreigners who are known for really immersing themselves in and speaking Lithuanian fluently are those who come to gain converts, such as the Mormons or other groups.

Lithuanians can generally speak a few other languages. Many people in their thirties say that they learned Polish by watching television, even though it is completely unrelated. Lithuanians have a strained relationship with their Slavic neighbors, and complicated feelings about speaking Polish and, especially, Russian. It is not uncommon to see Poles visiting Vilnius, speaking Polish to Lithuanians, and referring to the city by its Polish name, Wilno. In the same way, Russians will speak Russian and refuse even to try to communicate a few words in Lithuanian. Such behavior is very irritating, as it assumes some kind of claim to the country. However, if a foreigner makes it apparent that there is no alternative, Lithuanians will gladly oblige by speaking any common language that can be found. Older people are the most reluctant to speak Russian, and may even be openly rude to those who approach them speaking Russian. But a quick "Excuse me, but I don't speak Lithuanian" will usually be enough to have them coming around to answer your questions or help you find your way. The bottom line is that it is not the language that is bothersome: it is any sort of posturing.

Young people are less likely to have strong feelings about speaking Russian, although usually they are not completely fluent in the language as it is no longer compulsory in schools. Those under thirty usually relish the opportunity of trying out their English, German, or French skills on native speakers. Most Lithuanian children start learning a foreign language at school in the second grade, at the age of about seven; the language taught is at the school's discretion, and most schools teach English primarily; however, German and French are also popular options. In the sixth grade students learn yet another foreign language. Some schools teach Swedish or Latin.

THINGS TO SAY

Do you speak English?	*Ar jus kalbate angliškai?*
Yes/No	*Taip/Ne*
I don't speak Lithuanian	*Aš nekalbu lietuviškai.*
Please	*Prašom*
Thank you	*Ačiū*
Excuse me (sorry)	*Atsiprašau*
Good-day	*Laba diena*
Good-bye	*Viso gero*
See you later	*Iki*

Everything is *Gerai*

Gerai means good—and much more. *Viskas gerai* is a phrase that means "everything is okay." Very few Lithuanian conversations will not have this expression in them. However, being told *viskas gerai* does not necessarily mean that everything is okay. It is the same as receiving the answer "Fine" to the English question, "How are you doing?" It is a white lie often told to others. The phrase can also be used to stop a conversation that is getting uncomfortable. If a debate is getting heated a peacemaker might concede that both sides have a point and that both can be seen, rendering the situation as *viskas gerai*.

Swearing

Lithuanian swearwords on the whole lack punch. Most compare people to animals. It is generally accepted that people from the Žemaitija region have the most colorful swearing vocabulary—the strength of which precludes it being written, let alone translated, in this book. Often in conversation Russian or English swearwords will make an appearance, as Russians especially are known for their creative and innovative cursing. Sometimes the Russian words will have a Lithuanian ending placed on them.

"Bad language," as in most parts of the world, is usually indicative of a lower class, but among friends in Lithuania swearing is relatively common, especially among men. Those serving in the military tend to have very extensive vocabularies of both abusive and salacious terms.

GESTURES

Lithuanians are not effusive in conversation, but do a great deal of leaning forward and head nodding when speaking. If explaining something procedural they will use their fingers to count out the steps. Counting starts with an outstretched hand where the smallest finger is brought into the palm by the opposite hand's index finger. The opposite hand's index finger will push in the adjacent fingers until it reaches the thumb.

Lithuanians also use gestures as shorthand. Using one's index finger and thumb and flicking it against the Adam's apple is way of saying that either the speaker or someone else is drunk. Spitting over one's left shoulder three times is used to ward off bad luck when someone has said something that arouses superstitious beliefs. Other common gestures show that you think another person is stupid. Taking one's index finger and knocking it against one's head repeatedly, or placing the index finger against one's temple and using a circular motion, or knocking one's knuckles across one's head followed by knocking the knuckles against a hard surface, preferably wood, are all ways of saying that someone is lacking in intellect.

GETTING TO THE POINT

Certain pleasantries are seen as false. Asking how people are doing and if everything is okay is considered unnecessary and sometimes even mildly obnoxious. Lithuanians are direct in that "please" and "thank you" are not tacked on to many requests. Foreigners will sometimes feel that a demand has been made when in fact a Lithuanian has merely requested something. Also much of the Lithuanian language is based on tone of voice, so one will ask sweetly for a particular object but use a phrase such as "Give me that book," and once the book is handed over will respond with a "thank you." However, keep in mind that while saying "thank you" is important, once is usually sufficient. Lithuanians are sincere, and one genuine "thank you" is all that is needed to show gratitude.

Social context is reflected in Lithuanian forms of address. When addressing another person there are two forms of "you." The informal form of "you" is *Tu* and the formal form is *Jūs*. There are also the terms *Ponas* and *Ponia*, which are polite forms of address for a man and a woman, respectively. They are used when speaking to people whose names you do not know, and are similar to Sir and Madam in English.

WHAT IS FUNNY?

Lithuanian humor is one of those things you either get or don't. It is mostly dark, tends to favor long or absurd jokes, but also has a playfulness about it. Jokes that are grossly hyperbolic or deliberately underestimate another's capabilities or the outside world are considered quite funny. For example, if a person with a cold is asked how their health is, quips such as "I will survive until spring," or "Don't get excited, I am not dying!" or "I'm planning on living until I get my pension," are all fine responses. Making people seem foolish or ashamed is not particularly frowned upon.

Love Note
In the office one day, an American worker rushed in to show his colleagues an anonymous text in Lithuanian he had received on his cell phone saying, "I love you." At the time the "I love you" Internet virus was doing the rounds. The women in the office conferred in Lithuanian, which the American did not understand, and told him that his cell phone was no longer safe to be used and had to be buried so that it would not infect other phones. The alarmed owner believed them—to be informed hours later by the grinning trio that it had been a practical joke.

Lithuanians enjoy language jokes, using puns and word play. They often mesh Western European, Polish, or Russian words together to create a joke in the context of a particular situation, as each language carries its own dynamic weight. For example, to use a Polish or a Russian word in a regular Lithuanian conversation is to draw attention to something. Thus a dig at a person would be to call them *Vilenskas*, meaning they are in Vilnius but, as it is the Polish version of the word, that they are appearing to be "too Polish looking" and not Lithuanian enough. As Poles are seen as zealous, asking someone if they went to church, using the Polish word, is another overlay on a joke that implies they are being too religious. This love of mixing up words leads to the Lithuanian custom of quoting movies. Long chunks of dialogue are well-known and memorized. A great number of these lines tend to be from Russian movies.

Lithuanians, for all their melancholy and romanticism, also love deflating ceremony or ostentation. Some say that their refusal to take ceremony seriously is partly a reaction against Soviet times. For example, in 1982 when the Soviet leader Leonid Ilyich Brezhnev died no announcement was made for thirty-six hours; however, the programming on radio and television changed almost immediately. Only sad music was played on the radio, and ballets such as *Giselle* and *Swan Lake* were shown on TV. None of this came with any explanation, so the public knew that something sad had occurred, just not exactly what. The absurdism of previous times gives Lithuanians a special appreciation of jokes that poke fun at the idea of ceremony for inexplicable reasons.

SERVICES
Mail
Lietuvos paštas is the country's postal service provider. The Lithuanian postal service marks its foundation as 1918, as it wasn't until 1917 that correspondence was allowed in the Lithuanian language, following the German occupation in the First World

War. During both the Tsarist Russian and Soviet occupations the postal service was run by the authorities in Moscow. The first stamp of independent Lithuania was issued on October 7, 1990.

International express mail companies such as DHL, FedEx, and UPS have offices in the large cities. Visits to the post office can seem like a step back in time, as many are in older buildings that have been left unrenovated. Some of the clerks staffing the counters also behave as if they are still working under a Soviet system, where providing service is not that important. The Lithuanian postal system is reliable and relatively cheap, which is useful should you have more souvenirs than room in your baggage. Postcards and standard letters can be mailed within the country and abroad within a 1–4 litas price range.

Post offices are also places where bills can be paid. Gas, electricity, landline telephone, and cell phone bills are just some of the payments that can be made at a local post office. However, many Lithuanians are choosing not to wait in line, and to make electronic bill payments or set up automatic transfers from their accounts.

Telephones

The state-owned Lietuvos Telekomas was responsible for all the fixed lines in the country until 2003, when the market was opened up to competitors; the company renamed itself and now is referred to as TEO. Upgrades to the phone system are continuous and fiber-optic cable is being used in parts of the country's phone network. Connections are either perfectly clear or fair, depending on whether you are in a highly populated urban area or in a small rural town.

Public telephones (*taksofonas*) require the purchase of a card (*telefono kortelė*) in order to make a call. Cards can be purchased at kiosks and inside post offices; they are also usually available in corner shops that sell sundries. Cards come in denominations of 9, 13, 16, and 90 litas . It is possible to make overseas calls from public telephones, but these phones are often not well shielded from street noise and do not have seating, making long conversations less than comfortable.

Calling within the country and from abroad is slightly confusing. For example, if you are in Vilnius and calling another landline number in Vilnius then you only need to dial the seven-digit number. When calling from one city code to another on a landline, you must first dial 8, wait for the tone, then dial the city code and the number. With cell phones the situation is slightly more convoluted, as all Lithuanian cell phone numbers begin with 86. When calling a Lithuanian cell phone from abroad, drop the initial 8 so that the number begins with 6. Otherwise, when using cell phones within the country, keep the initial 8 when dialing.

TELEPHONE CODES

The international code for Lithuania is 370

Vilnius 5

Kaunas 37

Klaipéda 46

Šiauliai 41

Druskininkai 313

Palanga 460

Nida 469

A Mobile Country

Walk through the streets of any major Lithuanian city and you will see that everyone is talking or texting on a cell phone (*mobiliakas*). In fact, most young Lithuanians use text-messaging almost exclusively as it is very cheap. Even children as young as ten can be seen with cell phones. Many Lithuanians have gone from households with one landline to every household member owning their own cell phone. As the jump was fast, certain items such as pagers never made it into the country in a significant way, and other things such as voice mail or answering machines are rarely used. In fact, if you have an answering machine, be prepared for Lithuanian friends to leave somewhat uncomfortable messages stating that they would like to speak to you and not some machine. Your voice mail messages will also go unchecked, so it is best to call back and try to speak to someone. For those visiting Lithuania for an extended period, a good investment is to purchase a SIM card from one of the three major cell phone companies: Bite, Omnitel, or Tele 2.

Internet

Most young people are computer savvy, and after Independence the country bounded into the technological age with great promise. Many young urban Lithuanians now work abroad as computer programmers and designers. According to a 2006 survey about 40 percent of the country as a whole uses the Internet, with 1,073,611 visitors between the ages of fifteen and seventy-four using it at least once a month. The average time spent per viewer was fourteen hours in a month, with 991 page views.

The online research company Gemius conducted a survey of the most popular Web sites in Lithuania in 2005 and found that a news portal, delphi.lt, was the most visited site. As PCs are still a bit pricey, averaging about US $1,000, many users in Lithuania access the Internet via their cell phones. In major cities there are a number of free Wi-Fi hot spots. Most large towns have at least a few Internet cafés. Costs usually run about $1–2 an hour for accessing the Internet in such places.

THE MEDIA

The majority of city dwellers rely on the radio for news in the mornings on their drive to work. During the day the Internet is the place to skim the headlines. Almost all Lithuanians who own a television watch the evening news to catch up with the day's events.

Television

Many American sitcoms have made their way into Lithuania, so although they are taught British English in school Lithuanians often use American catchphrases and slang—and are more aware of American life as it is presented in TV shows. Visitors staying in hotels will usually have access to BBC World, CNN, and Sky News as their only sources of information in English. All international programming is dubbed. Latin American soap operas have a strange popularity and are shown in the early morning hours. Many people watch these programs as they are getting ready for work.

There are eight basic, or broadcast, channels, two state-owned, and six others. The state-owned channels are LTV and LTV2. The two major commercial channels are LNK and TV3. LNK is an acronym for Laisvas ir Nepriklausomas Kanalas (Free and Independent Channel). The station was founded in 1995 and hosts an array of mostly original programming geared toward a Lithuanian audience. TV3 was launched in April 1993 and carries a variety of its own original programming coupled with American TV shows.

Press

The two biggest press agencies are BNS, the Baltic News Service, which covers all three countries, and the Vilnius-based Lithuanian news

agency ELTA. BNS is
considered the more reliable of
the two. Major cities all have
their own newspapers, which are
read avidly. *Lietuvos rytas* is the

biggest daily newspaper in the country, with
Respublika trailing in second place. Both feature
larger Saturday editions, which many Lithuanians
enjoy reading over a cup of coffee. The most
reliable business daily is *Verslo Žinios*.
Newspapers tend to have a political preference
rather than a hard-line slant. *Lietuvos rytas* is
slightly right-wing, whereas *Respublika* claims to
be more firmly in the middle than its slightly
leftist copy would warrant. The right-wing paper
Lietuvos Aidas is not popular or widely read.

There are a few English-language publications.
The weekly *Baltic Times* covers all three Baltic
countries. *City Paper* is a magazine run out of
Tallinn that covers news and events along with
editorials in all three Baltic capitals. The bimonthly
Lithuanian Business Review covers topics in the
Lithuanian markets. The small, but excellent *In
Your Pocket* guide series, which started in Vilnius,
publishes its hometown's event listings and
editorials, along with (usually irreverent) reviews
of the city's establishments. The magazine also
covers all major destinations in the country.

Radio
Besides the state-owned Lithuanian Radio and
Television (LRT), both national and local stations

exist. For the most part pop music reigns on FM stations. Lithuanians will have music blaring at all times: in the car, at the lakes in summer, or sometimes even in the office. However, the radio isn't the main way of getting information. It serves more as ambient—although usually very loud—noise. The BBC World Service can be tuned in at 95.5 FM.

CONCLUSION

In Lithuania communication is a vital part of the traveler's experience. You may need to put a bit more effort into first meetings than you are accustomed to, but the result will be some amazing conversations. The rewards of visiting this country are great: the startling natural beauty; the feeling in the major cities that change is occurring right before you; and the forging of true friendships after formality falls away.

The Lithuanians are bold in business and loyal in friendship; in academia they are clear and intelligent thinkers; and over history they have shown courage and resilience. They wear these virtues lightly—reticence and quirky humor are part of their appeal.

If Lithuania touches its visitors it is with a softly sung and occasionally bittersweet ballad informed by a rhapsodic take on life—the feeling that can master a person overlooking the Curonian dunes, watching the sea consume the sun setting over the pier at Palanga, or listening to an impromptu performance by Vilnius street musicians. Lithuania is a country where artists in a small section of the capital declare a republic and the city smiles and allows them their fun. A place where one can be working in an office, and within hours be in the middle of a forest watching men leap over bonfires and girls wearing candled wreaths. It is a place where a man will collect rocks to exhibit in an outdoor museum that people actually visit; where someone will gather together statues from Soviet times and display them in an idyllic country setting. It is a land that many have entered to claim as their own before being driven out.

The country that has changed hands so many times has settled into peace and prosperity. Its people are ambitious for a better future, but still spend sunny weekends by the lakes enjoying the simple pleasures of life. And it is in these quieter moments, when family and friends are sitting and talking over food and drink, that it is clear that to most Lithuanians the future looks bright.

Further Reading

General

Aleksa, Osvaldas. *Lithuania: A First Week*. Vilnius: Baltos lankos, 2005.

Bousfield, Jonathan. *The Rough Guide to the Baltic States*. New York: Rough Guide, Ltd., 2004.

Jankevičiūtė, Giedrė. *Lithuania*. Vilnius: R. Paknio liedykla, 2006.

Kairienė, Audra. *Lithuania. Nature, Traditions, Culture, Cities*. Vilnius: R. Paknio leidykla, 2006.

Venclova, Tomas. *Vilnius*. Vilnius: R. Paknio liedykla, 2004.

Williams, Roger (ed.). I*nsight Guides Baltic State*s. London: APA Publications, 2005.

Žukauskas, Ramūnas. *Lithuanian Food*. Vilnius: Baltos lankos, 2005.

History

Kiaupa, Zigmantas.*The History of Lithuania*. Vilnius: Baltos lankos, 2005.

Kuodytė, Dalia and Rokas Tracevskis. *The Unknown War: Armed Anti-Soviet Resistance in Lithuania in 1944-1953*. Vilnius: Genocide and Resistance Research Centre of Lithuania, 2004.

———. *Siberia: Mass Deportations from Lithuania to the USSR*. Vilnius: Genocide and Resistance Research Centre of Lithuania, 2005.

Jewish Interest

Greenbaum, Masha. *The Jews of Lithuania: A History of a Remarkable Community 1316–1945*. Jerusalem: Gefen Publishing House, 1995.

Katz, Dovid. *Lithuanian Jewish Culture*. Vilnius: Baltos lankos, 2004.

culture smart! lithuania

Index

Acknowledgments

I would like to thank Renata Šutovaįtė for her friendship, help, and all the philosophical chats we had no matter the hour. Vikis Satkevičius deserves praise for providing the best in Vilnius airport pickup services and being a dear friend. Special thanks to my father, George, who made countless meals for me so I could sit writing for hours—and to Liz, Catherine, and Anna for their support in all my endeavors. Lesser thanks to Lucy Andruha, Siofra Byrne, Evelyn Kay, Michele Alexia, Ciara Byrne, and Alana Cotter for inviting me to do fun things when I was supposed to be writing this book!